Studying in the UK:
A guide for international students

Cerys Evans

2nd edition

Studying in the UK: A Guide for International Students

This second edition published in 2012 by Trotman Publishing,
a division of Crimson Publishing Ltd, Westminster House, Kew
Road, Richmond, Surrey TW9 2ND

First edition published 2011

© Trotman Publishing 2012

Author: Cerys Evans

British Library Cataloguing in Publication Data
A catalogue record for this book is available from the British
Library

ISBN 978 1 84455 521 5

Designed by Andy Prior

Typeset by IDSUK (DataConnection) Ltd
Printed and bound in the UK by Ashford Colour Press,
Gosport, Hants

Contents

Contents

Contents

Acknowledgements

I would like to thank the students who shared their stories of studying in the UK, thereby helping others to learn from their experiences. I am grateful to all the university and college staff who generously gave their time to help me. Particular thanks are due to Mim Woolley of Sheffield College, Jessica Guiver of York St John University and Lauren Welch and the team at the US-UK Fulbright Commission. Thank you to the Scottish Credit and Qualifications Framework Partnership for allowing use of an excerpt from the framework diagram.

Finally, I would like to show my appreciation to my family and friends for all their practical and moral support during the writing of this book.

Map of the United Kingdom

Introduction

Studying overseas can have great benefits personally, academically and economically, but it takes careful research and thorough preparation to get the most out of the experience. Getting to grips with a new system of education, and often a new language of study, far from your support network of family, friends and community, can be a daunting task. This book is aimed at any EU or international student who may be considering studying in the United Kingdom, at further education, undergraduate or postgraduate level. Whether you are reading this in your home country or you are already here in the UK, it will help you to make the most of the experience.

The book is a guide to studying in the UK. It will introduce you to the education system, take you through the process of choosing a course, support you through the application process and provide you with information on fees and funding. It is full of tips from fellow international students who have already asked all of the questions you may be asking now. You can benefit from their experiences and learn from their mistakes. You can also find out the many advantages that they attribute to studying in the UK.

There are many benefits to studying abroad, particularly in these competitive times when you may be looking for a way to stand out. Employers and universities look for applicants with the best education and skills. Exposure to new courses, a new language or a different culture offers great opportunities for you to develop as an individual. You are more likely to be adaptable and have a broader range of experiences, which will be valued by employers who know the importance of an international perspective – not to mention the personal benefits in developing your independence and world view. It is highly likely that overseas study will change your life.

So why choose the UK? The UK has a great tradition of learning and academic excellence: it is the home of some of the oldest and best universities in the world, offering internationally renowned qualifications. You can be sure that your institution will have been checked thoroughly for the quality of its provision. Students in the UK develop a set of skills they can transfer into a range of different settings, whether it be further study, research or work.

Studying here provides you with the chance to perfect your English language skills in the home of the English language, a multicultural society with a rich heritage. The UK is a small nation full of diversity, offering history and tradition alongside the cutting edge of fashion, music and theatre. The climate is temperate, with warm summers and chilly winters, but nothing too extreme. The south of the country offers the warmest, sunniest weather, while the north is slightly cooler and wetter, but average temperatures only differ by a few degrees. The landscape is varied with beautiful coastlines, mountains, woodland and moors; picture-postcard villages, industrial towns and 24-hour cities.

The make-up of the United Kingdom

The UK has a population of over 62 million people and is made up of England, Scotland, Wales and Northern Ireland. Each country has its own separate identity while sharing an official language, currency and time zone. Although centrally governed by the national government in Westminster, each country retains some of its own powers of governance in Edinburgh (Scotland), Cardiff (Wales) and Belfast (Northern Ireland). Education systems across England, Wales and Northern Ireland tend to be broadly similar, while Scottish education features some differences that we will explore in the book (see p.13).

The largest of the four countries is England, which has a population of around 52 million and features some of the world's most renowned centres of learning. Over 7.8 million people live in the capital, London, which is home to a number of the UK's most prestigious universities. The rest of the country has much to enjoy and a lower cost of living than the capital. Check out www.enjoyengland.com for more information.

Scotland, to the north of the UK, has a population of around 5 million. It offers an ancient and respected tradition of learning and a flexible education system. Its mountainous Highlands are well worth a visit while its dozens of islands offer tranquillity, beauty and wildlife. The native language, Scots Gaelic, is spoken by a minority of Scottish people. Visit www.visitscotland.com to find out more.

With a population of 3 million and a landscape of green hills and valleys, Wales has much to offer, from heritage to creativity and culture. Although English is spoken everywhere, there is a strong movement to keep the native language, Welsh (Cymraeg), alive. See www.visitwales.com for further information.

The smallest in population is Northern Ireland. It has around 1.8 million residents and is a small, close-knit community. Its size means that everything you need is accessible. Northern Ireland is known for the friendliness of its people and its natural

beauty. The native language is Irish Gaeilge. Check out www.
discovernorthernireland.com.

Changes to education and immigration

A number of changes have taken place in the UK in the last year
or two. Tuition fees for home and EU higher education students
rose dramatically in England in 2012. On the positive side, the
systems in place in Scotland, Wales and Northern Ireland remain
far more favourable for EU students and in some cases are free.

The good news is that the rise in fees has not affected
international students. The increase is due to changes to
the way in which universities are funded, but it does not
apply to international students who are not subsidised by the
UK government.

Recent changes to the student visa system, however, have
affected international students, particularly the closure of the
post-study work route. Visa changes have also resulted in one
university losing its right to sponsor international students;
students affected by this ruling have been offered support to
find alternative study options. On the other hand, more students
now report that they find the visa application process speedy and
efficient. A further benefit is the introduction of more rigorous
checks on institutions to ensure quality provision and to
maintain the high standard of UK education.

If you want to study in the UK, you need to know about the
education system, the fees and how to apply for a course and
a visa. The greatest choice involves what and where to study.
However daunting the task of discovering the ideal course at
an institution that suits you perfectly, it is an achievable aim.
The internet is full of information for international students, but

in order to avoid information overload you need to know what is important and who to trust. This book will help you discover this. Give yourself time and take the process step by step, using the chapters of the book as a guide and the starting point for your research.

Note

Throughout the book you'll find terms highlighted in bold. These terms are explained in the glossary at the end of the book. This glossary will help you to get to grips with terms related to studying in the UK.

Chapter 1

The education system in the UK

Many students will have heard about the world-class reputation of UK qualifications before they apply to study here. Students in the UK have the opportunity to think for themselves, to work independently and to maximise their academic potential. You could be studying in an institution with an ancient history combined with cutting-edge research; a city university with 40,000 students or a rural college with just a few hundred; studying purely academic subjects or achieving vocational excellence.

Education in the UK demands that students ask questions, discuss and analyse. Students are encouraged to work independently and to take responsibility for their own work. Your academic studies should develop your critical and analytical thinking and your research skills. You will have the chance to get involved in other activities in order to develop the range of skills valued by employers. The good news is that plenty of support is available alongside the opportunity for independent study.

With so many students in the UK coming from overseas, colleges and universities have a range of support services available, including international offices, students' union welfare staff, academic support staff, counsellors and advisers. These staff are here to make you feel at home in the UK and to help you adjust to life and study in a new country. Most institutions have an international office, advice centre or students' union, and you can contact their staff before you apply. If you attend an institution without such support services, you can use the services of **UKCISA** (UK Council for International Student Affairs); their website is packed with useful information and you can call them if you need further advice. The website is www.ukcisa.org.uk/student or you can telephone +44 (0)20 7107 9922.

The school system in the UK

At schools in the UK, pupils move up each year based on age, rather than ability. Compulsory schooling ends at age 16 with the completion of **GCSEs** (or **Standard Grades** in Scotland). The majority of students intending to proceed to university from England, Wales and Northern Ireland then go on to sit exams called **A levels** over two years, offering depth of study in a few subjects.In Scotland, pupils sit **Higher** examinations, offering greater breadth of study: this is more typical of Scottish education. These can be completed in one year, enabling progression to university aged just 17. Some students in Scotland continue into a second year of study when they start new subjects or take **Advanced Higher** examinations; these are more comparable to A levels.There is a range of alternative qualifications available across the UK, including the **International Baccalaureate**, **Cambridge Pre-U,** the Welsh Baccalaureate and more vocational, work-focused qualifications such as diplomas.

Qualifications across the UK are compatible with one another, although you will find that the system in Scotland is distinct from that in the rest of the UK.

The academic year

The academic year in the UK starts in September and finishes the following June or July. Universities tend to start in late September and finish earlier than schools and colleges. International students may be offered the chance to take preparatory courses before mainstream courses commence. Alternatively, there may be the opportunity to start a course at another time of the year.

Most universities and colleges have three terms divided by holidays at Christmas, Easter and the summer break. Your studies may be affected by bank holidays, most notably one day in early May and one in late May, when educational establishments close. For study purposes, universities divide their academic year into two semesters, with semester 1 running from September to January and semester 2 from late January to late May. Exams tend to be held at the end of each semester – both in January and in May or June.

Higher education (another name for university-level study) includes courses such as Foundation degrees, undergraduate degrees and postgraduate degrees.

Further education is offered below degree level to students who have finished compulsory schooling. It includes courses such as A levels, **BTEC diplomas** or **Access to Higher Education (HE) diplomas** (which provide a route to university for mature students).

The selection process for universities

Universities provide information on the minimum grades acceptable for entry through their websites and prospectuses, and these grades are used to select potential candidates. The grades required vary between universities and courses. In addition to achieving specific grades at A level or an equivalent standard, applicants to university have to demonstrate their ability in English and maths, normally gaining at least **GCSE** grade C or the equivalent. Certain courses require specific subjects as preparation for university, so students need to choose their qualifications wisely. For many professional or vocational courses (for example, medicine or physiotherapy) relevant experience, often gained on a voluntary basis, is essential. Students from the UK usually apply to university before they have completed their current studies, so much of the selection process is based on predicted grades, with places confirmed when results come out in August.

International applicants will be asked to achieve equivalent standards in order to be considered; you can discuss these with your college or university. So, an undergraduate course will require at least 13 years of education and qualifications comparable to A levels. Staff recruiting to a master's degree would be looking for a first or 2.i from your bachelor's degree in a related subject. If your academic qualifications or level of English are not at the desired level, you may need to consider further education, a Foundation year or an English course to prepare.

As part of the **Bologna Process**, university qualifications gained in the UK are compatible with those from other institutions in the European Higher Education Area, while strengths such as the autonomy and flexibility of UK education are maintained. This process allows for mobility in the international system of higher education.

If you plan to continue your studies elsewhere in the European Higher Education Area, you will need to know how many **ECTS** (European Credit Transfer System) points you will gain from your UK education. As a general rule, a three-year UK bachelor's degree carries 180 ECTS points, while a one year master's degree should be worth 90 ECTS points.

English language qualifications

All UK students have to prove that they have a basic command of English in order to cope with the academic demands of the education system. To cope with studying in the UK, you will also need to ensure that your level of English meets the required standards. You will need to achieve certain scores from specific qualifications in order to meet the entry requirements of your chosen course and the visa requirements.

> **❝** I have continued to enjoy studying in my second language. Sometimes I miss some complicated words when I am trying to translate, but I have learned to ask every time I don't understand. It is better to ask and look silly for one minute than not say anything and look silly every time I get it wrong.**❞**
>
> *Andrzej Polewaik, Poland.*

For the requirements of the **Tier 4** visa application (the points-based immigration route for non-EU students), if you are not from a majority English-speaking country and you will be studying a course below bachelor's degree level, you would normally need to demonstrate your competence in English by achieving level B1 at least on the Common European Framework of Reference for Languages (**CEFR**) in reading, writing, speaking and listening. This should be done through a Secure English Language Test.

For further details of the latest accepted qualifications and the contact details to arrange approved tests, you should go to the Home Office website at www.ukba.homeoffice.gov.uk and search for 'approved English tests'.

The following qualifications are currently approved as meeting the requirements of the **UK Border Agency** at level B1, although there is an ongoing discussion around qualifications and their comparisons to the CEFR, so it is important to check the latest information with the UK Border Agency at www.ukba. homeoffice.gov.uk.

- **IELTS**: Listening 4, Speaking 4, Reading 4, Writing 4 (4.0 overall).
- **TOEFL iBT**: Listening 9, Speaking 16, Reading 4, Writing 13.
- **PTE**: Listening 36, Speaking 36, Reading 36, Writing 36.

Other qualifications currently considered to be at a comparable level include University of Cambridge **ESOL** examination courses such as Cambridge English Preliminary (**PET**) and Cambridge English: Business Preliminary. To meet the requirements you would need to achieve an overall pass or pass with merit; in addition, all elements (listening, speaking, reading and writing) should be at borderline level.

For undergraduate courses (**QCF** level 6 or **SCQF** level 9 and above; see the following qualifications framework on page 9), students must have achieved level B2 in reading, writing, speaking and listening on the CEFR.

- IELTS: Listening 5.5, Speaking 5.5, Reading 5.5, Writing 5.5 (5.5 overall).
- TOEFL iBT: Listening 17, Speaking 20, Reading 18, Writing 17.
- PTE: Listening 51, Speaking 51, Reading 51, Writing 51.

A range of additional qualifications are accepted and the requirements can change, so you should check with the UK Border Agency for the latest information. UK Border Agency Officers will be able to refuse a potential student at the border who cannot speak without an interpreter.

In practice, the level of English required by your university is likely to be higher than the level required to meet visa requirements. Some institutions have their own tests in place to ensure that you will cope with the demands of their course. The exact scores required vary between institutions, but, as a general guide, the **British Council** suggests the following:

- further education: IELTS 4.5–5
- Higher National Diploma/Foundation degree/Diploma of Higher Education: IELTS 5.5–6
- bachelor's degree: IELTS 6–6.5
- master's degree: IELTS 7
- PhD: IELTS 6.5–7.

Some bachelor's degrees now require IELTS scores of 6.5 or above.

Equivalence of overseas qualifications

Before you can join the UK education system, you need to find out which level you should be studying at. You can do this by checking the equivalent of your previous education. In order to check the validity of overseas qualifications for UK-based study, institutions and individuals can use the services of **UK NARIC**. This national agency, managed on behalf of the government, is responsible for providing information and advice on vocational, academic and professional skills and qualifications from over 180 countries worldwide. UK NARIC, for a fee, will compare your qualifications with those in the UK and provide you with official documentation indicating your level of achievement. The institution where you apply may be able to provide you with information about whether your qualifications are acceptable, based on your original certificate and an official translation of your certificate into English.

Qualifications in the UK

The range of qualifications in the UK, often with similar names, acronyms or abbreviations, can be mind-boggling. The Qualifications and Credit Framework (**QCF**) and National Qualifications Framework (**NQF**) in England, Wales and Northern Ireland and the Framework for Higher Education Qualifications (**FHEQ**) will help you to determine the level at which you are studying. Scotland uses the Scottish Credit and Qualifications Framework (SCQF). Only accredited qualifications are included, so you can be sure that these qualifications are of high quality and meet the needs of individuals and potential employers.

Excerpt from the Qualifications Framework for England, Wales and Northern Ireland

Level	Examples of NQF/ QCF qualifications	Examples of FHEQ qualifications
2	GCSEs grades A*–C	
3	A levels International Baccalaureate BTEC diplomas, certificates and awards at Level 3	
4		Certificates of Higher Education Higher National Certificates
5		Diplomas of Higher Education Foundation degrees Higher National Diploma
6		Bachelor's degrees Bachelor's degrees with honours Graduate certificates Graduate diplomas
7		Master's degrees Postgraduate certificates Postgraduate diplomas
8		Doctoral degrees

© Crown copyright www.direct.gov.uk

Excerpt from Scottish Credit and Qualifications Framework Diagram

Level	Scottish Qualifications Authority qualifications	Qualifications of higher education institutions
6	Higher	
7	Advanced Higher Scottish Baccalaureate Higher National Certificate	Certificate of Higher Education
8	Higher National Diploma	Diploma of Higher Education
9		Bachelor's degree (ordinary) Graduate diplomas Graduate certificates
10		Bachelor's degrees with honours Graduate diplomas Graduate certificates
11		Master's degrees Postgraduate certificates Postgraduate diplomas
12		Doctoral degrees

© Crown copyright SCQF Partnership

Pre-university qualifications

Some form of pre-university study may be required if you need to bridge the gap between your existing qualifications and university study at level 6 on the Framework for Higher Education Qualifications. These courses could include language courses, further education or preparatory courses. You can study these in further education colleges or private language schools, or as a preparatory programme at a university. Courses in these settings are likely to be more supported and to require less independent study than those at undergraduate level or above.

For those requiring a Tier 4 visa, any academic or vocational study will need to be full-time and at level 3 or above on the National Qualifications Framework for England, Wales and Northern Ireland (level 6 or above on the Scottish Credit and Qualifications Framework – see previous tables). This rule may prevent you from taking certain vocational options (plumbing, brickwork, hairdressing and so on) that require students to commence their studies below level 3.

If you are looking for pre-university study, you may come across some of the following qualifications.

Access to Higher Education (HE) Diploma (or Access courses)

Access to HE courses are aimed at adults planning to progress to university but who left school without the usual qualifications, such as A levels.

Foundation programme

Foundation programmes are normally one year long and taken at colleges or universities to prepare for university-level study. Some Foundation programmes are designed to prepare you for study at a specific university. Foundation programmes that are aimed specifically at international students will also offer English language study.

Higher National Certificate (HNC) and Higher National Diploma (HND)

HNCs and HNDs are vocational higher education qualifications designed to give you the skills to apply your knowledge effectively in a particular job. HNCs normally take one year to complete full-time, while HNDs take two years full-time.

How is a Foundation programme different from a Foundation degree?

A Foundation programme is a course aimed at students who need to enhance their qualifications in order to get onto an undergraduate or postgraduate degree. Courses designed for students from overseas will often include the study of English.

A Foundation degree is a qualification in its own right, combining academic study with work-related learning and designed with a specific area of work in mind. You would study for two years full-time, with the option to 'top up' to a full undergraduate degree with further study.

Undergraduate qualifications

The first degree you work towards at university is known as an undergraduate degree. The term 'undergraduate' can also be used to refer to a student working towards their first degree. Undergraduate qualifications include bachelor's degrees, graduate certificates and diplomas. A graduate is someone who has successfully completed their first degree.

Undergraduate study generally takes three years on a full-time basis in England, Wales and Northern Ireland, shorter than the four year courses on offer in a number of countries. In most cases, you'll need to decide on one degree subject to specialise in, but a combination of compulsory and optional modules should give you some freedom to tailor your degree to your own interests and career aims. These modules tend to be related to your degree subject, rather than coming from a wide range of arts, humanities and sciences, for example. An alternative option is to study joint honours (often in two related subjects) or combined studies (choosing modules from a range of subjects but ultimately studying two subjects equally or majoring in one).

> When looking for colleges and universities online, you will find that UK educational establishments will have URLs ending in **.ac.uk**.

The following qualifications and their abbreviations are commonly used in UK higher education:

- Bachelor of Arts (BA)
- Bachelor of Science (BSc)
- Bachelor of Engineering (BEng)
- Bachelor of Education (BEd)
- Foundation degree (FDeg)
- Honours (Hons).

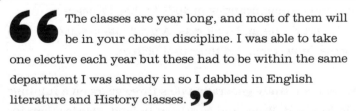

The classes are year long, and most of them will be in your chosen discipline. I was able to take one elective each year but these had to be within the same department I was already in so I dabbled in English literature and History classes.

Alexa Johnson, US

Scottish undergraduate study

Scottish undergraduate study tends to last for four years and to offer a broader, more flexible focus. It may be that you're not ready to focus on a single subject, or you want to study your chosen subject but with a broader perspective; you can choose to change the focus of your degree as you progress, with many students ending up with a degree that isn't the one they set out to achieve. Scotland has a history of learning dating back to ancient times; its four-year bachelor's degree system has gone on to be adopted by the US, Canada and Japan. It is so important for overseas students to make the right choices the first time, based on financial requirements and on the restrictions of the visa, although the Scottish system does allow more freedom than many of the courses on offer elsewhere in the UK.

> **“** I try to prepare students for the UK way of teaching and learning. For many of our international students, the way classes are taught and the way students are expected to learn are completely different from what they are used to: so different that many students really struggle until they come to grips with what is expected of them. Some lecturers are good about taking that into account, but others ... not so much. At my university we try to prepare them in advance during orientation week, with a British culture session and a 'how to study at a British university'-type session, but often it's a case of learning through experience. **”**
>
> *International officer*

Style of teaching and learning

You will find that teaching at universities in the UK may be quite different from teaching in your home country. Undergraduate study is made up of a combination of lectures, seminars, tutorials and, for science and engineering students, laboratory classes. In total you can expect to have around 15 hours of tutor contact time per week, although this tends to be less for arts and humanities students and more for scientists and engineers.

Lectures can be delivered to as many as several hundred students in the first year, although sizes tend to decrease in later years of study. Supporting the lecture programme are smaller seminars and tutorials which allow students to address the issues in greater depth, through discussion, analysis, problem solving or essay writing. Your ideas and opinions will be required and encouraged; you are expected to contribute and speak out. A key part of university is private study. A student can expect to spend a similar amount of time on self-study as on taught sessions. For academic guidance and support, you can turn to your tutor.

Universities vary and the systems in elite universities such as Oxford and Cambridge can be very different; it is important to research and understand these differences before you apply. University of Cambridge courses, for example, cover the subject very broadly in the initial years and then become more specialised and offer a wide range of options in the later years. Students at the University of Oxford apply for a three- or four-year degree in one to three subjects, studying those subjects exclusively, in depth and to a very advanced level.

Grading

The grading or classification of an undergraduate degree is based on the marks achieved through assessed work; your university will explain the weighting given to different assessments. Most graduates from UK universities are striving for an honours (Hons) degree, but a range of classifications are available:

- first class honours (1st)
- second class honours, upper division (2.i)
- second class honours, lower division (2.ii)
- third class honours (3rd)
- ordinary degree (pass)

In Scotland, four-year courses tend to gain honours, whereas a three-year course would be classed as an ordinary (or a general or designated) degree. In Scotland, some students choose to study the three-year ordinary degree as a qualification in its own right, whereas in the rest of the UK, most students gain an ordinary degree because they have been unsuccessful in achieving a degree with honours.

A first class honours degree is the highest classification achievable, with the exception of some highly rated universities, which offer even higher distinctions for small numbers of exceptional students.

There are some changes being made to the ways in which graduating students receive information about their achievements. Currently students receive their degree classification along with an academic transcript, but from 2013 more detailed information will be provided in the form of Higher Education Achievement Report (**HEAR**). In addition to degree classification, the new report will include the European Diploma Supplement, used across the European Higher Education Area (**EHEA**) to provide a recognised explanation of studies and their level, content and context. It is expected that the standard system of degree classification will continue for the immediate future, but that alternative systems of classification may develop over the coming years.

Postgraduate qualifications

Postgraduate study is further, more advanced study completed after graduating from university: i.e. postgraduate study is completed by graduates. Postgraduate qualifications include master's degrees, MBAs and PhDs. You might know postgraduate study as graduate study.

At postgraduate level, a taught master's degree in the UK will normally take one year, unlike the two years, or more, required in many other countries. This makes it an effective way to study, taking account of both time and money. Research degrees take slightly longer, from two years for the MPhil and from three years for a PhD.

Taught courses

- **Postgraduate certificates/diplomas:** Often leading to professional qualifications, these are shorter than master's degrees – four months for certificates and nine months for diplomas. They can be used as a progression route to a master's degree or offered as an alternative qualification, if a master's degree is not fully completed.
- **Master's degrees:** These include Master of Arts (MA), Master of Science (MSc), Master of Engineering (MEng), Master of Business Administration (MBA) and Master of Education (MEd). It is also possible to take a taught Master of Research (MRes) programme in certain subjects, where the majority of the course is based on a research project. Assessment for taught master's degrees is based on exams, course work and assessed project work.

Research-based courses

- **Master's degrees:** Research-based master's degrees include Master of Arts (MA), Master of Science (MSc) and so on. A Master of Philosophy (MPhil) is similar to

a PhD, but at a lower academic level, with much of the
assessment based on one large research project. Unlike
a traditional PhD, the MPhil is likely to include taught
units on research methods.

- **Doctoral degrees:**
  - Doctor of Philosophy qualifications (PhD or DPhil)
    require the preparation of new and original research
    presented as a **thesis** and defended at a *viva voce* (or
    oral examination). The entire PhD is often untaught,
    but supported by an academic supervisor.
  - The New Route PhD™ (or integrated PhD) offers
    taught activities and professional skills alongside
    supervised research.
  - Professional doctorates are available for those aiming
    for professional careers in areas such as business or
    engineering. These include taught programmes and
    integrate the academic and the professional.

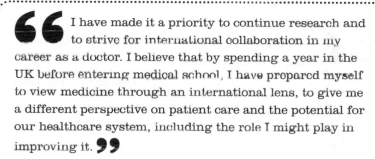

I have made it a priority to continue research and
to strive for international collaboration in my
career as a doctor. I believe that by spending a year in the
UK before entering medical school, I have prepared myself
to view medicine through an international lens, to give me
a different perspective on patient care and the potential for
our healthcare system, including the role I might play in
improving it.

Kimberly Stevensen, US

Style of teaching and learning

You will find that a taught master's degree offers a similar style
of teaching to an undergraduate programme, albeit at a higher
level. The main body of the course is led by lecturers and tutors,

with the option to specialise in your area of interest. You will be expected to develop a **dissertation** or research project, to demonstrate your skills as a student and researcher.

> At the end of a taught degree programme, you will normally be expected to produce an original piece of research known in the UK as a dissertation. At the end of a research-based degree, students will be expected to complete an original piece of research known as a thesis; the entire degree is often dedicated to preparing the thesis.

A research-based degree requires the completion of a major thesis. This is based on an individual research project that is carried out with the supervision of the university's academic staff. You may be able to take advantage of a taught preparatory course in research skills before you start a research-based master's programme.

The best thing about studying in the UK has been the quality of the education I have received. 99
Nick Casey, Australia

Grading

Postgraduate courses are graded as distinction, merit, pass or fail. Doctoral degrees tend to be graded as pass or fail only.

STUDENT STORY
Bola Phillips, Nigeria

Omobolanle Adunoluwa Phillips (Bola) is studying for the International Baccalaureate at Atlantic College in Wales, having completed her primary education in Nigeria and her secondary education in South Africa.

"I came to the UK to study for the experience. Moving from South Africa to here has been a big difference for me and the atmosphere in the UK is simply more to my liking. I have a lot of family here, so hearing their experiences from their schools got me quite interested. I wanted to go to a school with diversity and that's how I found Atlantic College."

Bola feels that she has grown as a person as a result of her time in the UK. "My experience here has been like no other. Having studied in two other countries in Africa it was nice to be in a completely different country and continent and experience the 'Western life', but at the same time have the opportunity to see how others live. Here I get the chance to meet people from countries that I had never even heard of. It is a once-in-a-lifetime opportunity to meet so many people from different countries, I really do appreciate it. Through it all, I have learned to be culturally sensitive and have respect for people in their different beliefs."

She has learned to adjust to the more independent style of study. "As far as the academic side of life, you are expected to be more independent in this school. At first I wasn't too optimistic about it, but now I have gained responsibility and have become more organised with everything that I do. Now I truly feel like a young adult."

Having been educated in Nigeria, Bola recognises some similarities in the style of education. "In Nigeria the majority of the schools actually go by the British system, especially if it is a private school. Private schools are expensive, but the costs which I pay here are still more expensive, especially because of the exchange rate."

Bola describes some of the practical sides of student life. "I guess the food is average, it has its good and bad days. I don't eat in the canteen often, but it really isn't that bad considering the budget we have. To be honest I am yet to attend a school where the food is spectacular."

"Accommodation is average: it's not the best but certainly not the worst that I've been in. It is four people per dorm and a general shower. There's a day room (a place where everyone can socialise without disturbing people who want to sleep or work) and there's also a quiet room where people work."

Bola has had no problems adjusting to life in the UK. "I come here often for holidays with family and friends, so it's more like an extended holiday, but with a lot of work!" Her sister had studied at the same institution before her, so she knew a little of what to expect. "My sister had graduated just before I came in 2010, and after hearing about her experience, Atlantic College seemed like the place for me: its diverse culture, the huge number of opportunities it had lined up for me and, most importantly, its attention to community service. In my country, Nigeria, there is very little or even no kind of community service provided in the schools. So this has also helped me to appreciate what I have, and also perceive the world from a completely different angle."

Bola's tips for other students considering UK study? "Stay focused and be determined."

Chapter 2
Universities

Which university should you entrust with your education? With 165 **higher education institutions** across the UK to choose from, many of them vastly different, it can be hard to make meaningful comparisons. When it comes to making a decision, it helps if you understand the different types of university in the UK. Looking at universities from a historical perspective is a good place to start, since most universities can be categorised according to when they were founded.

Categories of university

Ancient universities
The ancient universities are among the oldest in the UK (and among the oldest in the world), with teaching at the University of Oxford dating back to 1096.

- University of Aberdeen
- University of Cambridge
- University of Edinburgh
- University of Glasgow
- University of Oxford
- University of St Andrews

Red brick universities

These six universities were founded in the early 1900s in the industrial cities of England, as civic science and engineering colleges.

- University of Birmingham
- University of Bristol
- University of Leeds
- University of Liverpool
- University of Manchester
- University of Sheffield

Further universities followed, founded in the first half of the 20th century.

- University of Exeter
- University of Hull
- University of Leicester
- University of Nottingham
- University of Reading
- University of Southampton

Plate glass universities

The phrase 'plate glass' originates from the style of architecture, as the majority of these universities gained university status in the 1960s.

- Aston University
- University of Bath
- University of Bradford
- Brunel University
- City University
- Cranfield University
- University of East Anglia
- University of Essex
- Heriot-Watt University
- Keele University
- University of Kent
- Lancaster University
- Loughborough University
- University of Salford

- University of Stirling
- University of Strathclyde
- University of Surrey
- University of Sussex
- University of Warwick
- University of Ulster
- University of York

New (or post-1992) universities

Most of these universities started life as **polytechnics**, institutions of technical and vocational learning, so they tend to offer a more vocational, work-related range of qualifications. Their university status was awarded from 1992 onwards.

- University of Abertay, Dundee
- Anglia Ruskin University
- Bath Spa University
- University of Bedfordshire
- Birmingham City University
- University of Lincoln
- Liverpool Hope University
- Liverpool John Moores University
- London Metropolitan University
- London South Bank University
- University of Bolton
- Bournemouth University
- University of Brighton
- University of Central Lancashire
- Coventry University
- De Montfort University
- University of Derby
- University of East London
- Edge Hill University
- Edinburgh Napier University
- University of Glamorgan
- Glasgow Caledonian University
- University of Gloucestershire
- University of Greenwich
- University of Hertfordshire
- University of Huddersfield
- Kingston University
- Leeds Metropolitan University

- Manchester Metropolitan University
- Middlesex University
- University of Northampton
- Northumbria University
- Nottingham Trent University
- Oxford Brookes University
- University of Plymouth
- University of Portsmouth
- Robert Gordon University
- University of Roehampton
- Sheffield Hallam University
- Southampton Solent University
- Staffordshire University
- University of Sunderland
- Teesside University
- University of the West of England
- University of the West of Scotland
- University of West London (formerly Thames Valley University)
- University of Westminster Westminster
- University of Wolverhampton

Other institutions

Other UK institutions are not so easily categorised. The University of Buckingham is currently the UK's only private university although there are a handful of other private institutions that can award their own degrees. The Open University stands alone as the only distance learning university, while the University of London and UoW comprises many different, individual institutions. There have been a number of new institutions created from 2005 onwards. There are also a number of university colleges and colleges of higher education which are not officially recognised as universities, even though the university colleges can award their own degrees.

Private higher education

The UK does not have the same tradition of private higher education found in many other countries. As you have seen, there is one private university (University of Buckingham) and one university college (BPP University College), but the number of private institutions involved in the delivery of university education is growing. Some don't have the power to award their own degrees, so they work in partnership with other universities, from the UK and overseas. Example of institutions offering private higher education include Holborn College (Kaplan Financial), ifs School of Finance and New College of the Humanities.

The benefits of categorisation

Categorising institutions in this way may help you to make comparisons between similar ones. Universities created in a similar era will share some common features, which may result in a similar student experience. For example, many of the plate glass universities are campus universities, with university buildings, accommodation and facilities all on one site.

Many pre-1992 universities are considered to have a higher status than their more modern counterparts. Those universities chartered before 1992 tend to have more of a tradition of excellence in research, and thus often attract more international students. Consider the University of Oxford, offering traditional academic courses; it is world class in its reputation for research. It attracts the highest calibre of students and has large numbers of postgraduate students, many attracted from overseas. The newer universities, with their background of technical and vocational education, may do less research, but they often attract students from a wider range of backgrounds, including more local and mature students. Their entry requirements may be slightly lower and their courses may be more varied and have a vocational focus. Yet many of the newer universities are now pushing their way up the league tables in their quest for excellence.

University groups

There are different university groups that you may encounter
while carrying out your research. The following are groups of
universities that have banded together to share best practices or
to improve higher education by shaping public policy.

Russell Group

The **Russell Group** (www.russellgroup.ac.uk) represents 24
leading universities in their aim to maintain the best standards of
research and outstanding teaching. Most of the available research
grants go to universities in the Russell Group.

The current membership of the group is:

- University of Birmingham
- University of Bristol
- University of Cambridge
- Cardiff University
- Durham University
- University of Edinburgh
- University of Exeter
- University of Glasgow
- Imperial College London
- King's College London
- University of Leeds
  University of Liverpool
- London School of
  Economics and Political
  Science
- University of Manchester
- Newcastle University
- University of
  Nottingham
- University of Oxford
- Queen Mary, University
  of London
- Queen's University
  Belfast
- University of Sheffield
- University of
  Southampton
- University College
  London
- University of Warwick
- University of York

Getting a place at a Russell Group university is highly competitive. The group has published a paper for UK students encouraging them to choose their post-16 education wisely, in order to give themselves the best chance of a successful application to such competitive, academic universities. Although the paper focuses on UK qualifications, the information on subject choice is also useful to EU and international students, particularly if you haven't yet chosen your options for study at school. Visit www.russellgroup.ac.uk/informed-choices for more information.

1994 Group

The 1994 Group was established to promote excellence in research and teaching; the members work together to respond to key policy issues and share good methods and best practice. Representing 15 of the smaller research-based universities, the group consists of:

- University of Bath
- Birkbeck, University of London
- University of East Anglia
- University of Essex
- Goldsmiths, University of London
- Institute of Education, University of London
- Royal Holloway, University of London

- Lancaster University
- University of Leicester
- Loughborough University
- University of Reading
- University of St Andrews
- School of Oriental and African Studies
- University of Surrey
- University of Sussex

Visit www.1994group.ac.uk for more information.

> **❝** I had decided on the course I wanted to do before picking the right university. However, the subjects offered influenced my choice when picking the right course at the right institution. **❞**
>
> *Cynthia Cheah, Malaysia*

University Alliance

The University Alliance (www.unialliance.ac.uk) comprises 23 business-focussed universities with a commitment to innovation and enterprise. The alliance is made up of pre- and post-1992 universities with a range of backgrounds in research and teaching.

million+

million+ (www.millionplus.ac.uk) is a university think tank, a network of new universities working together to solve problems in higher education.

ukadia

Specialist art and design institutions from further and higher education have linked together to form the United Kingdom Arts and Design Institutions Association (ukadia; www.ukadia.ac.uk). Their purpose is to highlight their specialist provision nationally and internationally, as part of the UK's worldwide reputation in the creative industries.

Using university categorisations

Understanding the category or group that a particular university falls into will help you to make more significant comparisons and contrasts in your research, as well as giving you more insight into the university system.

The different types of university have their own strengths. Although the league tables rate some universities more highly than others, the more important question is whether the university suits you, your preferences, your style of learning and your future career or educational plans. Although status is important, if the institution is not right for you, then you will not benefit fully from the experience.

The information in this chapter is a starting point, but is not sufficient to determine where you should study; there are many other factors that you need to consider, and we will explore them in the chapter on choosing your course and institution (see p.45).

STUDENT CASE STUDY
Ami Jones, Hong Kong

Ami Jones defines herself as "slightly unusual for an international student". She is a British citizen, born in London with a British father, but, having lived in Hong Kong from the age of three, she is classed as an international student.

She describes coming to the UK to study as "an opportunity to come back home", but the UK wasn't the only country to be considered for her university studies. "Ultimately, in the private school environment in Hong Kong, the choice of country for higher education is basically between the US and Britain. As I have relatives, friends and roots here it just made sense to choose the UK. I also found that the British mindset and attitude were things I could relate to more easily; in contrast to America, I found it more grounded, self-deprecating and sincere.

"I didn't decide what I wanted to study until relatively late. At first I was sure I wanted to go into psychology, and thought about applying to study PPS (politics, psychology and sociology) at Cambridge. I later came to the realisation that, when I considered my talents and abilities, as well as what interested me, English was the natural choice."

Ami gained a place to read English at Sidney Sussex College, University of Cambridge. "As you can probably guess by the institution I finally went to, reputation had a lot to do with my choice, but location came into it as well. At the end of the day, Durham just seemed too remote and far north for me, so I didn't apply in the end."

She found the UCAS process fairly straightforward. "The UK application process is surprisingly efficient, especially when you compare it with the American system. You still have to reduce yourself to an essay and some figures, but the British system is straightforward and honest in stating that it is only interested in the raw, hard academics of each applicant; the pressure to come across as a 'rounded person' in the American application system – you need to be an excellent student but also an ace at violin while being captain of the basketball team – is getting a bit ridiculous."

As a British citizen, Ami didn't need to apply for a student visa, nor did she require too much assistance from her institution. "Cambridge was helpful enough, but as I was already somewhat familiar with the UK I didn't really stretch them by asking for much assistance." She explains that the cost of study in the UK is significantly higher than in Hong Kong, with academic fees alone three times more expensive.

She did encounter some challenges adjusting to British culture. "British culture is very odd, even to someone raised in a Western environment. Listen and observe as much as you can, or even watch British television to familiarise yourself. Comedy shows are a good way to tap into the British psyche. Surprisingly, the cultural adjustment has been the most tricky aspect for me. Perhaps because I have clearly been raised in a Western environment, it is taken for granted that I simply understand the quirks of British culture. It's not too bad, but it still does feel a bit like an inside joke I just don't get when I socialise with others."

Ami has some top tips for other students on the practical aspects of UK student life. "It sounds basic and silly, but food is something you'll be experiencing three times a day and more. I was lucky to get a college that serves affordable and tasty food. Of course it's not the most important thing, but do consider it when applying."

When adjusting to a new currency, she suggests operating in your home currency for as long as you need to. "Even when you think you've fully adjusted to the GBP system, you're probably still underestimating the value, so keep converting in your head whenever you buy."

Barking & Dagenham College

Barking & Dagenham College

An award-winning college very close to London

Do you want to go to an award winning college which is just a short train ride from the Tower of London, Buckingham Palace and Big Ben? Then come and study with us.

At Barking & Dagenham College we welcome students from all over the world. We offer hundreds of full-time courses for all ages and across a wide range of subjects from accounting to acting, business studies to beauty therapy, plumbing to photography, engineering to health and social care and so much more.

Our Higher Education programme offers Higher National Certificate (Level 5) qualifications right through to degrees (Level 6) and a post-graduate Master of Business Administration (Level 7).

Why should you study at Barking & Dagenham College?

1. We provide a range of high quality courses that support a worldwide job market. We also have excellent on-campus resources including a library and computer clusters to help you with your studies.
2. We know that it can be daunting to come to a new country to study and that is why we do our best to make you feel comfortable. You will receive support from our expert tutors and our Learner Help Centre.
3. We have an established programme of extracurricular activities to help you relax and make new friends.
4. We are very close to excellent transport links that can take you into Central London in 20 minutes, where there is an abundance

of resources to help you study and places to visit. Trains generally run until midnight.

5. We are award winning. In November 2011 we were presented with the Times Educational Supplement's "Outstanding entrepreneurship in learning and skills" award for the emphasis we put on giving our students real work experience, providing you with the work-ready skills that employers value.

Case Study

Sahil Saini has travelled almost 4,000 miles to study Business at Barking & Dagenham College.

21-year-old Sahil left Punjab over two years ago and is now in his third year studying Level 5 in a HND for Business; he is doing extremely well.

Sahil decided to study at Barking & Dagenham College after searching on the web for London Colleges.

Sahil said: "Ever since I started school I was always told that the best education in the world is in England. I always dreamt of visiting London and while I was online looking for a college near London I came across Barking & Dagenham College."

"I liked what I saw and decided to apply to study business. Everyone was really helpful as they understood that moving to a different country would be difficult but the whole process was very smooth and the dedicated International Team at the College were a great help and very supportive."

"Since I have started at College I have been made to feel very welcome and have had a great deal of support every step along the way. I have also made lots of friends as the College has a lot of social activities for everyone to get involved in."

"Before I moved to the UK I did not know anyone but it was a chance for me to stand alone and be independent which has been really rewarding. I would recommend Barking & Dagenham College to any other international students looking to study in the UK. It is a friendly college that can help you achieve your goals as I have done. Also having a qualification from the UK has worldwide recognition and will really help you get jobs in the future."

Sahil is now in his final year and is hoping to stay in the UK after College and begin his career as an accountant.

Chapter 3
Getting ready to research

This chapter outlines the information you need to know before you start your research into course and institution choice. It should provide an aid to safer research, as well as highlighting pointers to protect you when decision making.

> Try to avoid moving between different countries and education systems without first completing your current qualification. You may find that moving country mid-qualification will set you back with your studies, resulting in a longer and more costly period of study.

Safe research online

The internet allows you to investigate studying in the UK thoroughly, but you need to be sure that you are using reputable sources of information. All the websites included in the appendix to this book are current and reliable. As with all research, consider the perspective of the author when deciding how much importance to place on the information. There are many websites designed to make money from international students, but you should be able to access reliable information without having to pay for the privilege.

If you plan to use chat rooms to find out about UK study, make sure you use them safely. You may get offers of assistance which are genuine, but others may be looking to make money from you. As a reliable alternative, many universities offer reputable, moderated web chats, virtual tours and discussion forums.

Using an agent

Some applicants like to use the support of an agent when applying to study in the UK; this is your choice. You can use an agent, but you do not have to do so. A good agent can help you understand the UK education system and what level of study might be appropriate for you. The agent can help you apply for courses and support you in applying for a visa; they might offer support as you prepare to leave for the UK and while you are here.

> **❝** I applied through an agency, which I would highly recommend because it makes the whole process easier. The agency provided all the necessary forms for me to fill in and they sent it over for me. The longest part was to wait for a reply about application. Once I got my offer letter, everything moved pretty fast. **❞**
>
> *Cynthia Cheah, Malaysia*

As with all services, the quality of agents varies; some are very good, while others are considerably weaker. Some agents work on behalf of one or more institutions, while others are not linked to any specific one. Agents make money from fees and from institution commissions. Those linked to an institution may be paid a percentage of your tuition fees if they successfully place you there; it is worth remembering this if you feel yourself being steered towards a specific university or college.

Before you decide whether to use an agent's services, you should find out who they are linked to, how much they will charge you and what services they will provide. Make sure you fully understand what you are paying for.

Although the use of an agent can simplify the process and provide information on appropriate options that may improve your chances of a successful application, they cannot make the decision on behalf of the college or university, so they are not an absolute guarantee of success.

Finding a reputable English language course

As mentioned in Chapter 1, if you want to study in the UK you will have to ensure your level of English meets an acceptable standard. Often this will involve enrolling in an English language course before you begin your course in the UK. You should start to learn English in your home country initially, because you will need some skills in the language before you arrive; this will be particularly important if you need to obtain a visa or meet the entry requirements of certain courses. If you continue to study English in the UK, you will have the benefit of immersing yourself in the language and learning to communicate with first-language speakers with different regional accents. Whichever English course you choose, you will be encouraged to communicate and develop skills through a range of methods, including discussions, games and role play. You will work on your skills in reading, writing, speaking and listening.

There are hundreds of organisations offering a range of different English language courses, from English for business to English for academic purposes. It is important to choose an English course at a reputable centre. Choosing a course accredited by the

British Council means that you will be able to get help if you are dissatisfied with the course or the institution. It also means that you will gain a recognised qualification at a centre checked for its quality.

Accreditation UK, run by the British Council, externally checks English language teaching courses in the UK, including private language schools and programmes for children and young people. The council inspects providers in order to monitor and improve management, teaching, resources and welfare. The team makes regular inspections and some on-the-spot checks. This includes looking at what happens in the classroom, the quality of resources and how students are being taught. The scheme aims to maintain standards in English language teaching and to protect international students. You can find accredited courses through the English UK scheme at www.englishuk.com/en/students.

EU students may choose to access English for Speakers of Other Languages (ESOL) provision, which can offer different qualifications and may be cheaper. So how can you be sure that these courses are of an adequate standard? Public institutions offering ESOL provision are inspected regularly according to an inspection framework. Each country in the UK has its own inspection system:

- **England**: Ofsted: Office for Standards in Education, Children's Services and Skills (www.ofsted.gov.uk)
- **Scotland**: Education Scotland (www.educationscotland. gov.uk/inspectionandreview)
- **Wales**: Estyn (www.estyn.gov.uk)
- **Northern Ireland**: ETI, Education and Training Inspectorate (www.etini.gov.uk)

Do I need a Highly Trusted Sponsor?

When you start to research institutions and the visa process, you are likely to come across the term '**Highly Trusted Sponsor**' and you might wonder what it means. All applicants applying for a visa under the Tier 4 (points-based system) need a sponsor. The sponsor is simply the institution offering you a place on a course. Any institution wanting to recruit international students must be registered with the UK Border Agency and hold a Highly Trusted Sponsor licence. The licence is awarded to institutions with a reliable history of recruiting genuine students who follow the immigration rules in the UK. To find a list of sponsors, go to www.ukba.homeoffice.gov.uk/sitecontent/documents/employersandsponsors/pointsbasedsystem/registerofsponsorseducation.

How do I know if my college is legitimate?

Unfortunately, not all of the institutions you research online are genuine or reputable, and some may not even exist. As a student from overseas, you won't necessarily have the opportunity to visit your institution before you pay your deposit. This can put you at risk of signing up with a college or university that is not genuine. The British government takes the threat of bogus colleges very seriously and is working to crack down on private colleges suspected of being scams.

Even with the many quality checks in place in the UK, bogus colleges have been discovered and shut down in the past few years. The government is toughening up and making the checks even more stringent, including tightening up the rules around gaining a Highly Trusted Sponsor licence. In addition, institutions will need to become accredited by a statutory education inspection body by the end of 2012. All publicly funded colleges and universities in the UK are already inspected and accredited in this way, so you can be sure that they are genuine.

You can check if the English language school you are interested in is part of English UK by using the members' directory on their website, www.englishuk.com. Some private colleges are currently inspected by the British Accreditation Council (BAC), Accreditation Service for International Colleges (ASIC) and the Association of British Language Schools (ABLS).

As you would expect, the vast majority of private colleges in the UK are legitimate, with a number of benefits to be had from studying with them. The section on p.41 explores some of the advantages of private colleges. As with all of your educational choices, you should always make adequate checks to be sure that you are happy with the quality of any provision you are offered.

Use the list on the UK Border Agency website (listed on p.235) to search for a recognised sponsor. Inclusion on the list does not mean that the establishment has been accredited, simply that the institution is eligible to sponsor those applying for visas or entry clearance. Make sure that the name on the list exactly matches the name of the college where you are applying. There are many colleges that use similar names, often based on the good reputation of another similarly named institution. Many institutions use Oxford, Cambridge and London in their names; it doesn't mean they are based there, nor does it mean they have anything to do with those esteemed universities.

Although a good-quality website does not guarantee a genuine institution, a poor-quality website might suggest a poor-quality education provider. You may find that some bogus institutions feature websites containing spelling and grammatical errors, with inferior pictures or broken links to other sites. They may claim to be linked to a particular university or claim accreditation from an awarding body; follow this up by phoning or checking on the website of the awarding body or university, remembering to match the name exactly.

Remember, if it sounds too good to be true, it probably is. The price might be surprisingly reasonable or the entry criteria might be quite low; you may have the chance to complete your qualification much quicker than through other institutions. Sometimes a bogus institution might link itself to a fake awarding body or accreditation organisation, creating a cluster of illegitimate organisations. To check for a legitimate awarding body, use the Office of Qualifications and Examinations Regulation (**Ofqual**) website at www.ofqual.gov.uk. It features a list of regulated qualifications and awarding organisations.

Even if you are based in the UK and have a good understanding of the education system, it can be hard to determine whether a private college is genuine. Remember that most private colleges offer good quality, reliable education; by using these tips, you can reduce the risk of being deceived by a bogus college. Ofqual has useful information on its website at www.ofqual.gov.uk/help-and-support/166/308, including tips on how to avoid being taken in by a bogus college and what to do if you have fallen victim to one of these organisations.

Why choose a private college?

Some private colleges may be very similar to their public counterparts, but a significant number can provide a more unique or tailored experience; this can range from specialist subjects to specialist support. Many have a long history of catering for international students; indeed, international students might be the only students they deal with, so they may understand your needs very well. You could follow a university preparation programme at a tutorial or sixth-form college, sometimes leading to a guaranteed place at university. Other private colleges offer UK undergraduate and postgraduate qualifications in partnership with universities, but often at very reasonable prices. The colleges are recruiting students in an increasingly competitive marketplace; in order to succeed, they have to offer strong support and customer service, which should be of clear benefit to you (as a 'customer').

By now, you should be developing an understanding of the education system and the different types of qualifications and institutions available. You should know some of the ways to research safely and to find a genuine institution. Now is the right time to move on and start making some decisions about your education in the UK.

STUDENT STORY
Andrzej Polewiak, Poland

Andrzej Polewiak wasn't even thinking about studying in the UK when he came to London from his native Poland. "I originally came and worked in a hotel. After one year I decided to continue my studies and applied to London Met University, because it was nearby and because it had the kind of courses I was looking for in hospitality management.

"I did well at school and university carries high status in my country, so it was a proud moment for me and my family that I started university here. I still work part-time in the same hotel, so I can earn some money to help with my costs. It also means that I can truly understand what I learn at uni because I see it every day at work."

Luckily for Andrzej, he had got used to living in a new country before he even applied for university. "I was used to living in England before I started university, so I was able to adjust to life here before I adjusted to study. This was a good way to do things, so it was not too much to cope with all at the same time. I already rented an apartment with some workmates, so I decided not to move into university accommodation.

"I found the university application process was OK and didn't have any problems using UCAS. Applying for loans was a bit more difficult and I struggled to answer some of the questions. But I'm so glad that I filled it out because I got a loan to pay my fees. Because I came here as a migrant worker, I also got a loan and a grant to help with costs of living – I am very grateful for this and it helps me very much."

Andrzej's experience of UK study was not trouble-free. The first challenge to cope with was studying in a new language. "I always enjoyed learning English at school and I have continued to enjoy studying in my second language. Sometimes I can miss some complicated words when I am trying to translate, but I have learned to ask every time I don't understand. It is better to ask and look silly for one minute than not say anything and look silly every time I get it wrong."

Andrzej also found that he missed his family and his home country. "I was homesick when I first arrived and I still get homesick. I miss my mother and my brother and sister every day, even after I have been here for more than three years. I find it helps to keep busy, and because I study and work I am always very busy. I have met good friends who help me when I am feeling sad, some from UK, some from Europe and from the rest of the world. I have met some Polish friends and we cook for each other and celebrate special days."

He loves his adopted home. "I like England. London is great. It is so busy and exciting, particularly when you come from a small town. I have met some amazing people from all around the world. Unfortunately, it is so expensive, so even though I work I still have to be very careful with my money.

"I work out how much I will be spending every week on travel, food, bills etc, so I know exactly how much I have left. I don't have much money to socialise, but there are so many things you can do for free here, like parks, galleries, museums. You learn how to make your money go further, which is very important in life."

Although he has faced some challenges, Andrzej speaks very highly about the experience of studying in the UK. "The best things about studying in London are the diversity of the people I have met and the true friends I have made. I am so pleased that I chose to continue my studies here and my English is now much stronger, which is very important for hospitality work around the world. Studying here has changed my life. Next I plan to move to another country to work in hotels and perhaps postgraduate study – I just haven't decided where yet!"

Chapter 4
Choosing your course and institution

You can now turn your attention to making some choices about the education system and what it can offer you. There are numerous questions that you will need to ask yourself when deciding what and where to study. Choosing the right course and institution is essential, as changing midway through a course can be very difficult, particularly with all the bureaucracy surrounding a visa. You may have heard of some of the top universities and the best-recognised qualifications, but there can be a wealth of opportunities in a large number of colleges and universities; you just have to look.

> **❝** I wasn't able to visit the universities before I chose my course, so I simply read as much as I could about each of them. I knew I wanted to be in London, which was the perfect place for me to be as a creative writer, and I loved the look of the Greenwich campus. The programme sounded like what I was looking for as well. **❞**
>
> *Alexa Johnson, US*

How do I know what is right for me?

Studying requires a huge commitment of your time, energy and money, so you need to know that you are making the choices that will benefit you personally, academically and economically. You can go through all the quality checks available and check all the league tables and rankings, but that doesn't mean you are going to like the course or the university.

> The independent style that UK education is famous for extends to its support services. You may expect someone to tell you what to do when you go to them for advice, but they are more likely to provide you with information and support so that you can make your own decisions about your future plans.

Finding out the right choice for you is as much about knowing yourself as knowing what is available.

- What do you want to get out of the experience?
- What type of person are you?
- How do you prefer to learn?
- How do you prefer to be assessed?
- Are there specialist areas of interest you would like to study?
- Where do you want your study to lead?

A well-designed university website or a prospectus filled with smiling students on sunny days is only one side of the picture. Take any opportunities that you get to speak to tutors and students. Try to visit the institution or take advantage of events in your home country. Gather information and get advice from people you trust – teachers, advisers, parents or others who have studied abroad. Remember that courses and institutions change, so something that was true five or 10 years ago may well have changed by now. Entry requirements, courses, qualifications and staff can change from year to year. Try to keep in mind that one person's favourite course and highly recommended university will not necessarily be the same for you. This is your time to make a decision as an individual, so listen to others but consider what matters to you.

- Is it important that there are lots of students from your home country at your institution?
- What kind of support is available for international students?
- What kind of support is in place for students with disabilities?
- What kinds of social or cultural societies are there?
- Which sports can you get involved with?
- What are the accommodation choices and costs?

Fees and quality

Institutions charge a wide range of fees for their courses. You may be wondering whether paying the highest fees is the best guarantee of success – not necessarily. The highly rated universities that appear on international league tables and have a strong academic tradition tend to charge the highest fees, but there is not always a direct correlation between price and ratings. Some universities may choose to charge higher fees to boost their perceived status and appear more attractive to potential students. On the other hand, one or two of the institutions that appear in the *Times Higher Education Top 100 Universities* charge fees around the middle range. When making your choices, cost is an important factor, but most expensive doesn't always mean best, just as cheapest doesn't always mean worst. Remember to consider your other personal preferences when making your choices, rather than choosing a course based solely on the fees charged.

> **"** I think students should really be looking at the whole picture when deciding where to study. Not only should students be looking at the programme of study (making sure it's exactly what they want, looking at the faculty and its reputation, checking out the academic ranking or reputation of the institution), but they should also look at the facilities the institution provides, the location (big city, rural, small town), the size (huge student population could mean you'll be lost in the crowd) and, finally, fees and financial support. All of these things are equally important. If a student chooses an institution simply on academic reputation alone and does not look at where it's located, how big it is or what current students are saying about the support, then that student is missing out on a huge chunk of information that might make them think twice about applying. Choosing a university should be about making it the right 'fit' for the student, and a student should get a good feeling from all aspects of the university: then they know they are making the right choice. **"**
>
> *International officer*

Choosing your course

The most important choice is your academic subject, so you should decide on this first before searching for institutions offering the subject. Think about your interests and your career plans. If you are fairly clear about future career or educational plans, it can make sense to work backwards. For example, if you know you want to progress to a master's degree in biotechnology, it makes sense to choose a first degree in bioscience, chemistry, biochemistry or something similar. Think about what you hope to achieve and ensure that the choices you make will lead you to your end goal. If you will be returning to your home country after your studies, then you need to be sure that your qualifications will be recognised there.

If you are uncertain about your career plans, then consider your interests, the subjects you love and the things that inspire you. You could talk to staff at your current school or college about your strengths and your academic ability. If you are going to spend several years studying a subject, then you need to have clear reasons for wanting to study it. It certainly helps to have a love for the subject. There can be pressure to choose a mainstream profession with a clear career path, but many interesting and challenging opportunities can be found by studying subjects that are much less familiar. Many students find themselves pushed down a particular career path, only to change direction later on in life. Bear in mind that some courses will offer you flexibility through the choice of modules or options to change direction, as in the Scottish system, or by offering more than one major subject.

> **"** I didn't decide what I wanted to study until relatively late. At first I was sure I wanted to go into psychology . . . I later came to the realisation that, when I considered my talents and abilities, as well as what interested me, English was the natural choice. **"**
>
> *Ami Jones, Hong Kong*

Further education

Choosing a further education course is reasonably straightforward, in that the qualifications available are often fairly standard wherever you study. The modules within a BTEC Extended Diploma in Travel and Tourism, for example, will be similar wherever you choose to study them. It is a similar case with an English language course. The differences at this level are much more to do with the type of institution you choose and what they can offer you.

With pre-university study, you will need to check that the qualifications you choose will lead you where you want to go in life. If you plan to study history at a particular university, you need to check that your pre-university course will lead you there. Some colleges, both public and private, will have strong links with specific universities, offering a direct (and sometimes guaranteed) route. Start your search for courses at www. educationuk.org.

Undergraduate

Once you get to university level, more research is required. There is a much wider range of subjects, for a start – both vocational (relating to a job or broader job area) and academic. Many of the subjects may be new to you. The names of courses can be misleading, as two courses at two different institutions with the same course title can be hugely different. Higher education courses are written by the institutions, so the modules, the areas of specialism, the options and the methods of assessment will vary. You will need to look in detail, comparing and contrasting what the different courses have to offer and deciding what suits you best. Universities like to see that you understand their courses and what makes them different. Start your search for courses at www.ucas.com.

Postgraduate

At postgraduate level, consider how the subject you want to study complements your future plans. Think about whether you are looking for a taught or research-based programme. Check the content of the programme, including compulsory and optional units. The choices at this level are often based around checking the specialisms of the institution's staff and seeing how they match your own areas of interest. Make sure you meet the entry requirements; most institutions are looking for at least a 2.i from your first degree. You can start your search for opportunities at www.prospects.ac.uk, www.findamasters.com and www.findaphd.com.

> If you are looking to gain a professionally-recognised qualification like law, teaching or medicine, check that a UK certificate will satisfy the requirements of the professional organisation in the country where you wish to practise.

Choosing your institution

Once you have explored what you want to study and get out of the experience, the next step is to choose an institution. Your choice could range across the UK or even worldwide, or perhaps your choice of institution is dictated by where friends live or the finances you have available. Start thinking about what is important to you. To help with making your decision and narrowing down your choices, you might like to develop a series of questions to ask your shortlisted institutions.

Further education

Further education establishments vary in their size, specialisms and location, from large, vocational inner-city colleges to small, academic sixth forms. Ask what type of college they are, what kind of support you can expect and how they will help you with visa issues or to apply for further study. Are they experienced in supporting international students, or will you be only one of a handful? Entry criteria and fees vary, so make sure you can meet the entry and financial requirements. It pays to shop around, comparing what is on offer in relation to the fees you will be expected to pay. Don't forget to use a variety of sources in your research to gain a more balanced view.

Is the course of good quality?

The following bodies inspect provision in the UK's colleges and schools. They are independent organisations, free to inspect without bias or pressure. They talk to students, teachers and managers, checking quality and helping institutions strive for excellence. You can look at inspection reports for the institutions you are interested in, checking their grades and areas for improvement.

- Ofsted (England): www.ofsted.gov.uk
- Education Scotland (Scotland): www.educationscotland.gov.uk/inspectionandreview
- Estyn (Wales): www.estyn.gov.uk
- ETI (Education and Training Inspectorate; Northern Ireland): www.etini.gov.uk
- ISI (Independent Schools Inspectorate; UK): www.isi.net

Many private colleges are currently inspected by the bodies listed below; each one has its own processes to validate quality.

- British Accreditation Council (BAC): www.the-bac.org
- Accreditation Service for International Colleges (ASIC): www.asic.org.uk
- Association of British Language Schools (ABLS): www.abls.co.uk

By the end of 2012, all institutions will need to be inspected by a statutory education inspection body or work in partnership with a licensed sponsor.

Student satisfaction

You should also ask about the successes and satisfaction of previous students. Some colleges are better than others at recording and using this data. Most will carry out student satisfaction surveys, while some record where ex-students have progressed. Recommendations and word-of-mouth can be valuable ways of getting some insight into what is on offer. Finding out about other students' experiences might help you decide whether it is the right place for you.

Remember: it is acceptable for you to ask your shortlisted institutions these questions. You need to know that you are making a wise investment in your future.

> **66** My sister had graduated just before I came in 2010 and, hearing about her experience, Atlantic College seemed like the place for me: its diverse culture, the huge number of opportunities it had lined up for me, and, most importantly, its attention to community service. **99**
>
> *Bola Phillips, Nigeria*

Undergraduate and postgraduate

The first and most important question when choosing a university is: "What matters to you?"

Are you looking for an experience at an ancient university or are you happiest in a modern, city-centre university? Does it matter to you whether your university has 200 students or 20,000? Perhaps the collegiate system at Durham, Oxford or Cambridge would give you the benefits of a large university with the community feel of a smaller college. Do you want to be at a campus university, with lectures, services, accommodation and entertainment all in one place? Is research quality important to you? What about reputation? Would you prefer to continue with your postgraduate studies at the same institution, or are there benefits in moving?

> ❝ Make an informed decision about what degree and what university to go for. Get as much information as possible. Don't be afraid to contact universities directly and ask for extra information. If possible, attend an open day or arrange a private visit. ❞
>
> *David Stoll, Luxembourg*

Which are the best universities?

There are a number of league tables ranking universities, each using slightly different criteria and weighting the criteria differently. Criteria used include data on research quality, student satisfaction and how much is spent on facilities, as well as entry standards and completion rates. When deciding how much importance to place on a league table, you need to know what criteria are being used and how they are being used, and consider how relevant the results are to your decision making.

There are a number of downsides to the league table system. There is a risk in placing high importance on current rankings that might have changed considerably by the time you have finished your course. The universities know the criteria, so they can make decisions that bolster their position but may mean little to you as an individual. An upgrade of all the ICT facilities might help to boost a place in the league table, but does it matter to you if you use your own laptop?

It makes sense to consider the rankings as a rough guide, rather than considering them your most important piece of information. Subject tables are often more revealing than the ranking of a university as a whole, so take a look at how your department is rated within these tables.

> 66 For my chosen course, pharmacology, I searched for the top 20 universities for the subject and picked from that list. I also visited these universities during open days, which was very helpful in deciding on my final choice. 99
>
> *Yana Dautova, Russia*

Take a look at the following league tables.

- The Complete University Guide
  www.thecompleteuniversityguide.co.uk
- *The Times*
  www.thetimes.co.uk (you will need to subscribe)
- The *Guardian*
  www.guardian.co.uk/education/universityguide
- THE World University Rankings
  www.timeshighereducation.co.uk/world-university-rankings
- QS World University Rankings®
  www.topuniversities.com

- Academic Ranking of World Universities www.arwu.org
- *Financial Times* Business School Rankings http://rankings.ft.com/businessschoolrankings/rankings

Is it a good quality course?

Responsibility for academic quality in the higher education sector lies with the individual institutions. Universities in the UK are independent and autonomous with their own quality systems, but they are not left entirely to their own devices. The Quality Assurance Agency for Higher Education (**QAA**) undertakes reviews and publishes reports, verifying how well the institutions are doing and highlighting good practices or ways to improve.

Other measures of quality include the Research Assessment Exercise (**RAE**), which is to become the Research Excellence Framework (**REF**) by 2014. This is the system for assessing the quality of research in the UK's higher education institutions. The system helps to decide the allocation of research funding and establish reputation. The quality of research is the most important factor in the assessment. The most recent results can be found at www.rae.ac.uk.

Take a look at the university's destination statistics. This will tell you where ex-students have moved on to – whether employment or further study. The downside of the data is that many students don't go immediately into relevant graduate work or study, but may do so after a break to travel or earn some money. On the positive side, it can be a good indicator of the relevance of your course to your chosen field. Remember to look at a range of students, not just the exceptional individuals. Ask your institution where to find this data.

You might use the recommendation of a friend to determine which institutions to consider, but have you thought about using the recommendations of thousands of students? iAgora (www. iagora.com/studies/United Kingdom) shares the opinions and experiences of international and exchange students in UK. The site allows students to rate their university in areas such as academic studies, housing, student life, expense and learning English. Alternatively, the Unistats website (http://unistats.direct. gov.uk) is an official website featuring the results of the National Student Survey. You can use it to compare universities and courses by checking out student satisfaction rates and looking at the percentage of students employed in a graduate job six months after completing their studies.

Entry criteria

When choosing a course, you need to be realistic about your own academic capabilities and make sure you can meet the entry requirements. If you are academically weaker than many of your fellow students, you are unlikely to find a place at the Universities of Oxford or Cambridge, but there may be many other universities that would suit you better. Talk to the institutions about the grades they require, and also about the grades that applicants normally apply with. There is likely to be strong competition for places at the most well-respected and popular institutions or courses. The minimum entry requirements listed in the prospectus might not be enough to gain a place, so it is important to be aware of this before you decide where to apply. Applying early can be beneficial.

Not just statistics

The factors that determine how much you get out of your education in the UK are based on more than simple statistics.

Many students talk about the feeling they get from being in an institution: perhaps its ethos and how its students and staff behave. Unfortunately, you can't get this from a website, so visiting an open day or a recruitment event in your home country can help. Don't forget that these events are mainly designed to sell the benefits of the institution, so it makes sense to compare a number of institutions if you can.

> **❝** No website can give you a clear picture of what the university is really like. Make sure you come and visit the institutions during open days – it is very useful. **❞**
>
> *Yana Dautova, Russia*

Whether an institution is right for you depends on what you need and expect from that institution. Consider support services, location, transport links, facilities, how selective the institution is, numbers of undergraduate or postgraduate students, architecture, specialisms, sports and social events, access to places of worship, reputation, quality, whether you want to meet other students from your home country, how your subject will be taught and assessed, background of the lecturers and so on. Once you have gathered the information you need, you can start forming a shortlist of places where you might wish to study, in readiness for the application.

British College of Osteopathic Medicine

A world leader in osteopathic education

The British College of Osteopathic Medicine (BCOM) is internationally regarded as one of the world's best specialist osteopathic education institutions. Since its foundation in London in 1936 by the famous naturopathic osteopath, Stanley Lief, the College has become a world leader in osteopathic education and research. Based in Hampstead, North London, BCOM's friendly campus has the most full-time academic staff of any UK osteopathic college, and was the first institution in the UK to offer an osteopathic honours degree and to achieve a landmark "approval without conditions" QAA-led RQ recognition from the General Osteopathic Council. BCOM has been running its much-praised four-year undergraduate Master's in Osteopathy (M.Ost) since 2008, and is now validated by Plymonuh University.

Excellent facilities BCOM offers the most advanced osteopathic research facilities in Europe, being the only specialist college to provide cutting-edge on-site human-performance and hydrotherapy laboratory facilities. Founder of the International Conference on Advances in Osteopathic Research (ICAOR), BCOM fosters a strong research environment that enables advances to be disseminated more generally, with the best student research being presented at leading international conferences. It also works to instil a research ethos into BCOM graduates, increasing the clinical knowledge base and providing Continuing Professional Development.

BCOM's holistic osteopathic approach BCOM is particularly regarded for its uniquely holistic or naturopathic approach to osteopathic care, and works hard at promoting the philosophy, science and clinical application of holistic osteopathy and naturopathy within the UK and throughout the international community. BCOM's undergraduate and postgraduate students are an integral part of its teaching and research clinics.

Case study

A degree and a career

Recent graduate Byung-ho Kim is the first Korean osteopath to be trained in the UK. Known as Kim to colleagues and friends, he now practises osteopathy at a busy clinic in Seoul, South Korea, working with US chiropractors. Kim views his experience at BCOM as a great turning point in his life and was given support throughout his degree by staff and fellow students. Kim said of his experience studying at BCOM: "During my degree I found that osteopathy is not just a branch of medicine, osteopathy is a principle of medicine and a connection between general medicine and alternative or complementary medicine. BCOM has been extraordinary for me as a foreign student because of the family-like atmosphere."

Stephania Humphrey is a practicing Osteopath and Naturopath. After graduating from BCOM in 2010, Stephania set up in a GP practice in West London. Stephania then became an associate at a practice in South London, where she now works, as well as running her own private practice. Stephania's experience at BCOM was an extremely positive one and she was made to feel very welcome and supported, finding the course to be both intense and rewarding. On her time at BCOM, Stephania said: "The course helped me immensely with my career. I absolutely love being an osteopath and being part of this profession, and without BCOM I would not have been able to do what I enjoy most every day. There is no other degree like the one at BCOM: it is fun and rewarding and the years fly by, so enjoy it all while you are there! You meet people you will know and be friends with for life, and generally the people drawn to work in this profession all tend to be very caring and respectful individuals."

Contact Details

British College of Osteopathic Medicine, Lief House, 120-122 Finchley Road, London NW3 5HR; Tel: +44 (0)20 7435 6464; Email: admissions@bcom.ac.uk
www.bcom.ac.uk.

Chapter 5
Alternative options

Having researched the options available for study in the UK, you may feel that full-time UK-based study is not right for you. Perhaps you don't want to leave your family and friends for such a long time, or maybe the costs of studying and living in the UK will be prohibitive. Perhaps you feel more comfortable following the education system of your home country, but are still interested in living in the UK. There are a number of alternatives to studying full-time in the UK. Remember that these alternative options will have different implications for funding, qualifications, quality and visas than full-time UK-based study, so you will need to be sure you are aware of these differences.

> ❝ I came to the UK to study as part of the Fulbright Summer Institutes Programme. I was most interested in visiting the UK in order to gauge two different things: how education (especially science) differs from that of the US and how Americans were perceived outside of America. ❞
>
> *Tim Ohlsen, US*

Exchange programmes

Many UK institutions welcome students on study abroad, **Erasmus** or international exchange programmes. These programmes give students from international institutions the chance to experience UK study for a semester or two, or during the summer. There are variations in the different schemes in terms of fees, funding, academic credit and so on.

Exchange programmes are a low-risk way of experiencing international study, sometimes without the additional costs of overseas study. On the European Erasmus exchange programme, students continue to pay fees at the same rate as at their home institution. US Fulbright summer programmes offer funding to help cover costs. In cases where there are further costs, there may be scholarships available to help.

An exchange can give you the chance to test whether you would like to undertake a full course in the UK. You can strengthen your CV and your language skills, demonstrating adaptability and international awareness on an exchange. Students tend to gain academic credit, rather than a full qualification, from a UK institution.

Speak to your school, college or university to check out the possibilities; many universities have their own international exchange or study abroad offices. Alternatively, if you have a specific UK institution in mind, you could approach them directly to see if it will be feasible. The most appropriate sources of information are likely to be in your home country, but you can also try the following websites:

- www.britishcouncil.org/erasmus (EU)
- www.fulbright.co.uk (US).

The Erasmus Mundus scheme allows you to study joint master's and doctoral degrees across more than one European country. The programmes are open to students from across the world, not just Europe, and scholarships are available.

How about an International Master's in Russian, Central and East European Studies? Study year one at the University of Glasgow and, in the second year, choose from Estonia, Finland, Hungary, Poland or Kazakhstan.

Find out more about Erasmus Mundus at http://ec.europe. eu/education/external-relation-programmes/mundus.en.htm

Gaining a UK qualification in another country

The UK has a number of universities with overseas campuses, including:

- Nottingham University has branches in China and Malaysia
- Middlesex University has campuses in Mauritius and United Arab Emirates
- Manchester Business School has global centres in Hong Kong, UAE, Singapore, Brazil and China
- University College London has bases in Qatar, Kazakhstan and Australia
- University of Central Lancashire has a campus in Cyprus, with plans for a private university campus in Thailand
- University of Warwick is going to be part of New York University's super-campus in New York.

Some countries have education cities where international universities are represented. For example, Dubai International Academic City features partners from across the world; UK partners include University of Exeter, University of Bradford and Heriot-Watt University.

Other UK universities also work in close partnership with universities overseas. Attending such a setting can give you the chance to gain a UK qualification in your home country, or maybe somewhere where the fees or the cost of living is lower than in the UK, although your exposure to British culture and life will be limited.

The benefits might be financial or personal, allowing you to remain with your family and, in some cases, eliminating the need for a UK visa. You may be able to study part-time if this is not restricted by the requirements of a visa. EU students will need to investigate the financial and visa implications of studying outside the EU.

Check which institution will be awarding your qualification. A degree awarded by a UK university, even if gained in another country, still has to adhere to the same standards and is still inspected and assessed in the same ways.

For further information, go to www.educationuk.org/uk/article/uk-qualification-in-your-own-country.

> **❝** I decided to apply for the Erasmus programme. I had to pass both a written and oral exam so my teachers could check my level of English was good enough and that I had strong motivation to study abroad. **❞**
>
> *Erica Cancelli, Italy*

Gaining an international qualification in the UK

Conversely, some overseas (particularly US) universities have branches in the UK, often in London, allowing you to live in the UK for your studies while following the educational programme of another country. Some of these institutions offer the benefit of dually recognised qualifications. Institutions include Hult International Business School (www.hult.edu) and American InterContinental University (www.aiuniv.edu/London) from the US and Limkokwing University of Creative Technology (www.limkokwing.net) from Malaysia. You should be able to get information about these institutions and others in your home country. The Global Higher Education website features a list of universities with branch campuses overseas at www.globalhighered.org/branchcampuses.php

Distance learning

Perhaps you would prefer to study via distance or online learning. This can enable you to gain a UK qualification from the comfort of your own home, without the costs of moving to the UK. Remember that you will not be exposed to the full breadth of the UK educational experience. Distance learning requires focus and discipline; you will need to dedicate time to your studies without the structure of a timetable. For some people, distance learning can work very well, allowing them freedom and flexibility.

Many UK universities offer distance learning qualifications to international students. Ask them about distance learning, including costs, support, and the benefits and pitfalls of studying this way. The Open University is the only university in the UK dedicated to distance learning, with a wide range of courses available. The UK also has a number of private colleges offering distance learning provision.

To find out about choosing a distance learning course and for a list of accredited providers of distance learning, visit the Open and Distance Learning Quality Council (www.odlqc.org.uk). For options at university level, go to www.qaa.ac.uk. For information on the Open University, go to www.open.ac.uk.

According to the Higher Education Statistics Agency (**HESA**) in 2010/2011, 500,000 students gained UK higher education qualifications without necessarily setting foot in the country; that accounts for one in six of all enrolled students.

US student Tim Ohlsen attends the University of Pittsburgh, Pennsylvania. He came to the UK to study as part of the Fulbright Summer Institutes programme.

"I was most interested in visiting the UK in order to gauge two different things: how education (especially science) differs from that in the US, and also to experience the way Americans were perceived outside of America. I had spent a significant amount of time in East Asia previously, but when I moved across the States to attend college, I became a little more aware of the European influence on the East Coast. That in particular interested me enough to apply for the programme. The fact that the programme was also fully financed by the US/UK governments was also a factor; otherwise I doubt I could have afforded it."

Unfortunately, Tim's desire to understand how science was taught in the UK wasn't fulfilled. "I feel like the faculty were trying to teach the course in a way that would appeal to non-UK students more. Of course, it was still a good learning experience and I had quite a bit of fun."

He decided to study at Newcastle University based on its geographical location and on what the institution could offer. "I wanted to see all of the UK – the countryside, the coast, the Midlands, etc – not just London. I feared that if I were in London, I would be so preoccupied with the city that I might forget the rest of the UK, which has plenty to offer in its own right. With regards to Newcastle specifically, I was interested in the international summer school because it would expose me to students from all over the world (though mostly from the UK). It also seemed that Newcastle had an established biomedical science faculty who could make the classroom experience worthwhile as well."

Even before he arrived in the UK, Tim felt well supported by Newcastle University. "They advised me on how to travel to the airport, where I would be picked up in a taxi and taken to my accommodations. They also sent a welcome packet which was fairly helpful. I think I was as well or better prepared for arrival in Newcastle than I was when I first visited the University of Pittsburgh."

In spite of all this support, Tim's arrival in the UK did not go smoothly. "My flight was actually cancelled and then delayed nine hours in Paris. After deciphering a French phone card given to me by the airline (it seriously took an hour, as I don't speak any French), the university was relieved to be in contact with me, and fluid in altering their plans. Furthermore, when I lost my baggage, they were very helpful in taking the necessary steps to get it back as well as showing me places to purchase new clothes."

He has some advice for fellow students as they adjust to life in the UK. "I would remind students (especially those rowdy Americans) that the British tend to be more polite and reserved than they are. I remember too many occasions when my American friends (or I) drove the British mad with their constant talking and high volume. I noticed that the Americans and British have different sorts of topics that can be sensitive, so students should always be conscious of cultural differences.

"I feel like the stereotype of bland English food doesn't have much substance to it (the stereotype that is, not the food). It is possible that as a university student I didn't have as much access to a wide variety of foods, but I would warn students to be prepared for a smaller variety of options than they might have at home. I also blame the British for my newfound addiction to tea, which I drink with cream and a little bit of sugar. I have other friends who have also studied in the UK and they have all found that the experience led them to drink more tea.

"Since everything is so close together, travel was very easy. I really encourage as much travel as possible, because experiencing all of Britain's regional differences (Cockneys, Geordies, etc) was one of my favourite parts of the trip." Tim used lots of different ways to get a feel for the country he was visiting. "Walking around random (maybe not too random) streets, mastering the train lines, maybe using some taxis. The UK really has a lot to offer, in terms of history and variety. From the beautiful countryside to cultural urban centres, there is much more to the UK than what one single place, no matter how great it is, can offer. There's a certain pride and richness to it that I haven't found elsewhere. This may just be a very American thing to say, but I would advise students to take risks, experience new things, meet new people, and gain from the experience."

Tim spent some time pondering the differences between education in the UK and US. "I had a lot of fun thinking about this during the trip. The UK university system is much more specialised than it is in the United States. For example, the past term I had courses in biochemistry, neurophysiology, East Asian history, and Greek philosophy. In the UK this could never happen. On one hand, I believe that students in the UK graduate being more knowledgeable in their specific subjects than their American counterparts, though there is something to be said about the liberal-arts education offered by America as well (of course I have to defend it because I do it!)."

The best things about studying in the UK? "I might just sum it up in all the wonderful things I've already mentioned, and these are: travel, football, pubs, history, and the people."

Bath Academy

Your route to success

Bath Academy is a very successful private sixth-form college specialising in helping students progress to the top 20 UK universities through courses appropriate to the needs of individual students. Our aim is to give students the encouragement and individual support they need to achieve their goals.

Two-year A level programme

The most usual route to studying at a UK university – especially for the more competitive courses and high-ranking universities – is a two-year course specialising in three or four subjects. This programme is recommended for students who have successfully completed five GCSE subjects, or have completed junior high school or its equivalent, in their home countries.

18-month A level course

The 18-month intensive A level course starting in January is ideal for international students coming from countries whose school year ends in December and begins in January, and who do not wish to wait until September to begin their pre-university studies.

University Foundation Programme (UFP)

A one-year alternative to A levels, the UFP is a course designed for international applicants who have already completed their high school education. Over one academic year it provides students with the necessary English academic knowledge and skills to succeed in undergraduate study at a UK university.

GCSEs

These courses, for students aged 14+, are an excellent general education and provide students with the knowledge and skills necessary to be successful at A level.

English language courses

Students who wish to develop their knowledge and skills in English language can study general or intensive courses, or courses for professions such as law, dentistry or pharmacy, as well as preparing for recognised qualifications. www.bathacademy.co.uk

Case study

Viktoria Loeffler

Viktoria was awarded the Paul Kitchener Memorial Prize for the best Foundation Course student at the House of Lords on March 2012 by Baroness Perry of Southwark. She had enrolled at Bath Academy after successfully completing IGCSEs as well as both the International Baccalaureate Middle Years Programme and IB Diploma at St George's College, an English-medium school in Buenos Aires, Argentina. Subsequently, Viktoria and her family returned to Germany. In order to study a finance-related degree at a good UK university, Viktoria studied the University Foundation Programme, achieving grade A in all six modules. She impressed everyone with her single-mindedness as well as her ability to relate to other students from very different cultures. She is now studying Accounting, Finance and Economics at Liverpool University.

Anastasia Malysh

Stacey was born in Rostov on-Don and received her primary education in Russia. However, her family relocated to Australia and Stacey then went to the International Grammar School in Sydney. Wishing to study law at a good UK university, she came to Bath Academy and undertook three AS/A Levels in one year, achieving an A* grade in English literature, a grade A in history and grade B in psychology. Her flair for presenting detailed, engaging and vibrant essays and presentations demonstrated the outstanding qualities she possesses and displayed an overall quality of professionalism. Following her success at A Level she was awarded a place at Nottingham University to study law, as well as being awarded a High Achiever's Scholarship by the University.

Chapter 6
Making the application

Once you have narrowed down your choices, you can make a start on your application. Getting the application right is key. Some courses don't require an interview, so your application is your only chance to make a good impression. For those that do interview, your application will determine whether or not you make the shortlist. In either case, the application is very important.

The application process

The process differs slightly between further education, undergraduate study and postgraduate study. For the most part, further education and postgraduate institutions require direct applications on the institution's own application form; this means that you may need to make a number of different applications in order to be considered by different institutions. Full-time undergraduate study is largely co-ordinated by the Universities and Colleges Admissions Service (**UCAS**). This system has the benefit of requiring only one application, and has a limit of five choices, with only one personal statement needed for all choices.

Most applications will ask for the following information:

- personal details
- education and qualifications
- your chosen course(s) and institution(s)

- a personal statement, stating:
  - why you are applying
  - the experiences, skills and qualities you offer
- references.

The application and personal statement should be your own work; under no circumstances should you allow anyone else to write the application or personal statement for you.

When applying, the best thing is not to rush and to make sure that the choices are right. **99**

Nadya Pramudita, Indonesia

You can prepare yourself by compiling all your academic certificates from completion of compulsory school onwards (and official translations, if they are not in English). Give yourself time to get information from UK NARIC about the equivalent level of your qualifications. Make sure you have evidence of your level of English. See Chapter 1 on the UK education system for details of recognised English language tests (see p.5).

Further education

Most colleges will have their own application form and application process. If you are undecided about your institution you will have to make applications to each college, which can be time-consuming. Narrowing down your college choices to a shortlist before you apply will reduce the paperwork somewhat. The application process and timescale will vary between different institutions.

You will need to complete an application containing a personal statement. The colleges will want to know about you, your academic background, what you have to offer and what you hope to achieve. The information on personal statements for undergraduate study (see p.82) will be relevant. You can also contact your chosen college to discuss what they require from you. Colleges are likely to need copies of certificates, and official translations into English, for qualifications you have already completed.

Timescale

Some 12 to 18 months before you hope to begin your studies, start researching college choices and attending open days or recruitment events in your home country. Colleges work to their own application deadlines, but starting to make contact in the autumn term (around 10 to 12 months before the courses start) should give you time to apply.

Undergraduate

Applying for undergraduate study is focussed around the UCAS application process. There may be other aspects to consider, like admissions tests and interviews, but the UCAS application is an essential factor in your success; if you don't get the application right, then your brilliant score at the UKCAT test (see p.84 for more on admissions tests) becomes irrelevant and you won't make it to the interview stage.

You apply through a secure online system at www.ucas.com/ students/apply. Each applicant can make only one application per academic year for up to five choices of educational institutions. UCAS charges a processing fee of either £12 or £23 depending on the number of choices used. The applications are blind, meaning that each institution can see only what you've applied to study with them. There is no facility to indicate a preference of one institution over another; indeed, it is recommended that you do not show your preference in any way, so as not to disadvantage your application with other institutions. Any decisions about preference can be made once all the institutions have responded with any offers. After each university has made a decision and has responded, a firm choice (indicating where you wish to study) and an insurance choice or back-up option (in case you don't achieve the grades for the first) can be selected.

If you are yet to complete your studies, offers will be **conditional** on the achievement of certain grades. If you have completed all your studies you are more likely to be made an **unconditional offer**. Alternatively, applications can be classed as withdrawn or unsuccessful. See p.95 for more on offers.

> ❝ The UK application process is very efficient. At the end of the day, you still have to reduce yourself to an essay and some figures, but I appreciate how the British system is straightforward and honest in stating that it is only interested in the raw, hard academics of each applicant. ❞
>
> *Ami Jones, Hong Kong*

> ❝ I found the university application process was OK and didn't have any problems using UCAS. ❞
>
> *Andrzej Polewiak, Poland*

Applying for more than one type of subject area is not advisable. Your application – and your personal statement in particular – needs to show your commitment and dedication to your chosen area of study; it is almost impossible to show this effectively if you apply for a range of courses. For example, applying for biology and history courses could be hard to justify to an admissions tutor, whereas applying for biology and biomedical sciences is a more logical combination. You really need to decide on a subject before applying.

Timescale

About 18 months before courses start, you should be attending open days or recruitment events, finding out all you can about the courses and institutions. Using the information gathered, you can start to streamline your choices to a long list of contenders, before narrowing them down to the final five.

The UCAS system opens for registration from mid-June and the first applications are accepted from 1 September. There are three important deadline dates to consider if you are a home or EU student. UCAS needs to be in receipt of your application by the relevant date.

- **15 October:** The application deadline date for medicine, dentistry, veterinary medicine and veterinary science courses and all courses at the universities of Oxford and Cambridge.
- **15 January:** Deadline for all applications except those with 15 October or 24 March deadlines.
- **24 March:** Deadline for art and design courses, except those listed with a 15 January deadline.

Check university websites or the UCAS website to verify which date applies to your course. Applying in advance of the deadline can be beneficial, as many universities start processing the forms as they arrive, rather than waiting until the deadline date.

Deadlines for international applicants

Although international applicants have a little more flexibility, don't forget the deadline dates listed above. Overseas applicants must still meet the 15 October deadline for medicine, dentistry, veterinary medicine and veterinary science and for applications to Oxford and Cambridge.

In other cases, universities can consider an international application until 30 June, but there is no guarantee they will do so. The most popular courses are liable to fill up much earlier, so for the best chances of success, you should apply as early as you are able.

> UCAS is reviewing its admissions process, so the systems mentioned here may change but you shouldn't experience any differences for the next few years: nothing should change before 2016, with any proposed changes to be confirmed by 2014.

Deferring entry

Some applicants choose to defer entry for a year, applying during one application cycle but asking to be considered for the following intake. There is a box to tick to indicate this in the choices section on the application. All entry requirements will need to be met by the end of August, so deferred entry is not for those who need more time to meet the entry criteria. Some applicants defer in order to do something different for a year, such as travel, volunteer or work. It might be useful to defer if you are undertaking national service, as this will allow you to plan in advance for your studies. Deferred entry should be discussed with your institution before you apply.

How admissions tutors decide

Admissions tutors have a background in the subject for which they are recruiting. Increasingly, the admissions tutor will work with a team of assistants who are involved in the process of sifting and handling applications. The admissions tutor and team of staff make decisions on who to offer a place to, who to invite for interview and who to reject. They should base their decision on a set of clear, transparent entry criteria and guidelines; universities share information about their procedures and criteria on their websites. Universities (and their departments) may differ in the way in which they process applications. If your application is received by 15 January, universities should normally make their decisions by 31 March, but you may find that there is great variation in the time that it takes a university to respond.

> You can use only four choices for medicine, dentistry or veterinary medicine. The fifth choice must be used for an alternative course.

Admissions tutors have to offer places based on a target number of students. They should have a good understanding of the range of qualifications on offer, although they may work with staff from the international office when handling overseas applications. Despite the length of time you may spend perfecting your application, admissions tutors may spend only a few minutes reading it and making their decision. Don't give them a reason to reject you.

Admissions tutors make their decisions based on a range of factors:

- academic background, including subjects studied and grades achieved
- personal statement, to check the applicant's commitment to and understanding of the course
- strong academic references, indicating an applicant's strengths and approach to studies
- appropriate actual or predicted grades.

Your form needs to be:

- well presented
- free from spelling or grammatical errors
- completed in full
- accurate
- concise and succinct.

To improve your chance of getting offers, it is important to 'target' your application. Universities like to see that you are interested in them. Targeting your personal statement to reflect the particular specialisms of a university is a delicate balancing act; as much as you want to appeal to one institution, you do not want to deter the others. To target successfully, you will need to know as much as you can about the institution and department.

Personal statements

The personal statement is the only section of the UCAS application that allows you to write freely, albeit with a maximum of 4,000 characters or 47 lines of text. You should initially complete your statement as a word-processed document, before pasting it into the UCAS system. Don't waste space by unnecessarily repeating information that appears elsewhere on the form. It is likely to take time and several drafts to produce a statement that is suitable, so allow time to work on it and try not to get disheartened.

Talk to staff at your current educational establishment or at your chosen institution, and use the guidelines on the UCAS website. There is a vast amount of information online about preparing a perfect statement, but make sure you only refer to legitimate sites. The statement needs to be your own work. If you apply using content from another personal statement that has been submitted to UCAS or by using information gathered online, your plagiarism will be detected.

It is possible to buy a ready-made statement from the internet. *Don't do this*. The quality is questionable, it will never be a *personal* statement if someone else has written it, and UCAS's sophisticated plagiarism detection software means that you will get caught.

The personal statement is a formal piece of writing to demonstrate why the university should select you. The main focus of the piece should be academic. Although universities will want to know something about your general interests, the vast majority of the wording should be focused on why you want to study this course. Statements for vocational courses such as medicine or dentistry will often need to demonstrate more than just an academic commitment to the subject, so include relevant experience as a way to show this. The statement will be checked for content as well as for the standard of writing. Admissions tutors may also look at whether the statement and the academic reference match; is the referee describing the same person as the statement?

Your statement needs to be personal; this is what makes it interesting and different from the next applicant's. If a specific topic has confirmed your love for your chosen subject, tell the admissions tutor what it is. The piece needs to be analytical, not just descriptive; for example, write about what you have learned from your experiences rather than simply what you have done. Back up any assertions with examples. Don't forget the need to be clear and succinct; this is not a life story, it is a focused piece of academic writing. Feel free to use long words, as long as you use them in the correct context and they help to convey meaning, rather than detracting from it.

Aim to answer the following questions in your statement.

- **Why do you want to study this subject?** Why are you interested in the subject? What do you know about it? What does the course entail? What are you most looking forward to learning? Do you know where you want your studies to lead?
- **What makes you a suitable candidate?** What have you done that demonstrates that you are right for this course

or institution? Provide examples from your academic experiences and from elsewhere; perhaps you have read widely around your chosen subject or you can reflect on your work experience, volunteering or your interests.

- **What else do you have to offer?** What else will you bring to the university and the department? Are you a well-rounded person with a well-balanced life? You can reflect on hobbies, sports, achievements, positions of responsibility and so on. Consider how the skills you have developed in these other activities will help you at university.

EU and international students should also explain their reasons for wanting to study in the UK. If English is not your first language, it is helpful to refer to any evidence that demonstrates you are ready to study in English.

> The entry criteria listed on the website or in the prospectus are the minimum entry requirements. In selective institutions with far more applicants per place, meeting the minimum requirements alone is unlikely to guarantee success.

Admissions tests

Certain courses require applicants to take an admissions test in addition to meeting the entry requirements. Admissions tests are often a way to demonstrate aptitude rather than achievement, and help universities to choose fairly between highly qualified candidates. Many of the tests cannot be studied for, but sample papers and guides to the tests are available to help you prepare; preparation and practice are essential to success. It helps if you know what to expect and have had a chance to practise in a timed situation.

A range of different tests are available, and the results are used in different ways by different universities. Most tests have no opportunities for resitting and no pass or fail. The university you are applying to can tell you whether a test is required and, if so, which one. Some of the most widely used admissions tests are listed here, although their use as an entry requirement will change from time to time.

Subject-based tests

Medicine, dentistry, veterinary medicine and related courses

The BioMedical Admissions Test (BMAT) is required by:

- University of Cambridge
- Imperial College London
- University of Oxford
- Royal Veterinary College
- University College London.

The Graduate Medical School Admissions Test (GAMSAT) is required by:

- University of Nottingham
- Peninsula College of Medicine and Dentistry
- St George's, University of London
- Swansea University.

The Health Professions Admissions Test (HPAT) is required by:

- University of Ulster.

The UK Clinical Aptitude Test (UKCAT) is required by:

- University of Aberdeen
- Barts and The London School of Medicine and Dentistry
- Brighton and Sussex Medical School
- Cardiff University
- University of Dundee
- Durham University
- University of East Anglia
- University of Edinburgh
- University of Glasgow
- Hull York Medical School
- Imperial College London (graduate entry)
- Keele University
- King's College London
- University of Leeds
- University of Leicester
- University of Manchester
- University of Newcastle
- University of Nottingham
- Peninsula College of Medicine and Dentistry
- Queen Mary, University of London
- Queen's University Belfast
- University of Sheffield
- University of Southampton
- University of St Andrews
- St George's, University of London
- University of Warwick (graduate entry).

Law

The National Admissions Test for Law (LNAT) is required by:

- University of Birmingham
- University of Bristol
- Durham University
- University of Glasgow
- King's College London
- University of Manchester
- University of Nottingham
- University of Oxford
- University College London.

Mathematics

The Sixth Term Examination Papers (STEP) is required by:

- University of Cambridge
- University of Warwick

The following universities encourage applicants to take STEP:

- University of Bristol
- University of Bath
- University of Oxford
- Imperial College London

Tests for specific universities

University of Oxford

The following tests are required for admission to Oxford in the relevant subjects:

- Classics Admissions Test (CAT)
- English Literature Admissions Test (ELAT)
- History Aptitude Test (HAT)
- Mathematics Aptitude Test (MAT)
- Modern Languages and Linguistics Aptitude Tests (MLLAT)
- Physics Aptitude Test (PAT)
- Thinking Skills Assessment (TSA Oxford): for courses including geography, economics and management (E&M) and philosophy, politics and economics (PPE).

University of Cambridge

The following tests are required for admission to Cambridge in the relevant subjects:

- Modern and Medieval Languages Test (MML).
- Sixth Term Examination Paper (STEP) for admission to mathematics courses.

- Thinking Skills Assessment (TSA Cambridge): for courses including computer science, natural sciences and engineering at some colleges.

Registering for tests

Registering for a test is a separate process from the UCAS application. You will need to register early, as there will be limited dates available, particularly outside the UK. Registration for the majority of tests starts in the summer before applications are completed. There is a fee charged to enter for most tests.

The UCAS website has links to all the tests mentioned here at www.ucas.ac.uk/students/choosingcourses/admissions.

Applying to Oxford and Cambridge (Oxbridge)

An applicant can apply to either the University of Oxford or the University of Cambridge during an admissions cycle, but not both. Some courses are offered at one university but not the other. As at all universities, courses with similar titles may be very different in their content, so make sure you carry out detailed research.

In both cases, you are able to select a college within the university where you would prefer to study. Oxford and Cambridge also allow open applications where you don't select a college, although, if you are offered a place, you will not be able to change from the college you are offered.

Applicants to Cambridge living outside the EU need to complete a Cambridge Online Preliminary Application (COPA). If you want to be interviewed outside the UK, there may be an earlier deadline date to consider for both the COPA and UCAS application. Applicants wishing to be interviewed in India, for example, should submit the COPA by 9 September, closely followed by the UCAS application. Dates for other countries may vary so be sure to check. You will also need to complete an online Supplementary Application Questionnaire (SAQ) after you have applied through UCAS.

Both universities require certain applicants to provide examples of written work. For Oxford, the deadline is in early November. Applicants to Cambridge will be contacted with details of when to submit this information.

> ❝ As everything was done through UCAS, it was a fairly straightforward application process and I didn't encounter any problems. Applying for my postgraduate studies was even easier as it was handled directly by the university in question. ❞
>
> *David Stoll, Luxembourg*

Applying for postgraduate courses

Timescale

Research into your postgraduate choices ideally needs to start around 18 months before the programmes start, maybe longer if you are applying from overseas. Talk to the academic staff at your present institution – they may be able to advise on suitable universities or subjects. Make contact with the universities, checking entry requirements, closing dates and how to apply. Visit postgraduate recruitment events in your home country or the UK. See Chapter 7 on funding for information on finding money to study for a postgraduate degree.

From 12 months beforehand, you will need to start taking action and actually applying. Making individual applications to a number of universities can be time-consuming, so allow plenty of time to do so. In some cases, there is no formal deadline date, although applying early is recommended. Applications may take up to three months to be considered. An early application allows you time to concentrate on current studies, as well as allowing time to arrange visas or entry clearance and apply for funding.

Applications will often require a personal statement, so you could start to prepare this. Take your time to write an effective statement showing your understanding of and enthusiasm for the course, why you want to study at this university and what you hope to gain from the experience. At this point, if you are hoping to move into research, you may also need to work on your **research proposal**; this is a document specifying your area of proposed research and the rationale behind it.

Consider who you will ask to provide your academic reference and talk to them about it; you will require two or three referees. It is polite and to your benefit to discuss the request with them beforehand. In all cases you need to allow time for references to be written, obtained and added. Many an application has been delayed because a student can't get hold of their academic referee just before a deadline, so don't leave it until the last minute.

> 66 To apply I had to write a brief piece about my interest in the course and give three references for recommendations. One thing to note is that coordinating applications from overseas can be frustrating at times due to the time difference, so I suggest you start applying as early as possible to allow for this. 99
>
> *Kimberly Stevenson, US*

Which application service?

There is no single, central application service for postgraduate study and research. In most cases, applicants apply directly to a university, although a number of universities and professional courses do have their own systems. You can search for places across all the countries of the UK through Prospects, a useful website for undergraduate and postgraduate students, at www. prospects.ac.uk. Prospects also offers a service whereby you can apply for postgraduate opportunities at more than 70 institutions. If you apply to an institution that is part of the **UKPASS** scheme, the application will be forwarded to UKPASS.

UK Postgraduate Application and Statistical Service (UKPASS)

UKPASS (www.ukpass.ac.uk) helps universities to recruit students using a single online application system. Run by the team that provides UCAS, it offers a similar service to the undergraduate application system, although it is not universal. Although only 25 institutions (listed below) currently use the application service, you can still use the site to search for postgraduate opportunities at other institutions across the UK.

- University of Aberdeen
- Aberystwyth University
- University College Birmingham
- Buckinghamshire New University
- Christie's Education
- De Montfort University
- University of Dundee
- Edge Hill University
- University College Falmouth
- ifs School of Finance
- Institute of Education, University of London
- Islamic College for Advanced Studies
- The London College, UCK
- London South Bank University
- University of Northampton
- Oxford Brookes University

- Glasgow Caledonian University
- Glasgow School of Art
- Grimsby Institute of Further and Higher Education
- Ravensbourne College of Design and Communication
- University of Reading
- Roehampton University
- Royal Veterinary College
- University of Westminster
- University of Winchester

UKPASS does not have a specific deadline date, although individual universities may have their own deadlines. If you are in competition for a place, it can be beneficial to apply early. You can apply for a maximum of 10 choices. The institutions to which you are applying may charge an application fee.

Applying for professional courses

Certain professional courses have their own systems for processing applications.

Conservatoires UK Admissions Service (CUKAS)

Through **CUKAS** (www.cukas.ac.uk) you can search and apply for practice-based undergraduate and postgraduate music courses at the following **conservatoires**.

- Birmingham Conservatoire
- Leeds College of Music
- Royal College of Music
- Royal Northern College of Music
- Royal Conservatoire of Scotland
- Royal Welsh College of Music and Drama
- Trinity Laban Conservatoire of Music and Dance

You can register from early July, and applications should be sent by 1 October in order to be considered 'on time'. International applications may be considered by the Royal Conservatoire of Scotland up until 31 March. There are benefits to applying as soon as possible. Applicants can use up to six choices. Institutions can consider late registrations up until 31 August, although they are not obliged to do so.

Universities and Colleges Admissions Service (UCAS)

Although UCAS (www.ucas.com) primarily processes undergraduate applications, it also accepts applications for postgraduate social work and nursing courses. Apply through UCAS by the 15 January deadline for up to five choices. Many universities advise early application.

Graduate Teacher Training Registry (GTTR)

You should use **GTTR** (www.gttr.ac.uk) to apply for postgraduate teaching courses. Most institutions offering postgraduate teacher training are in the scheme; any that are not require direct application.

Primary teaching places are highly competitive, so you are advised to apply well in advance of the 1 December deadline. For secondary teaching, applicants have until the end of June, although popular courses can fill up by January, according to GTTR. You can apply for up to four courses.

Law Central Applications Board

There are differences in the ways in which students apply to legal postgraduate training in the four countries of the UK. You can find details on the relevant websites:

- England and Wales: www.lawcabs.ac.uk
- Scotland: www.lawscot.org.uk
- Northern Ireland: www.qub.ac.uk/schools/ InstituteofProfessionalLegalStudies.

Courses and universities that do not fall into any of the previous categories tend to require direct applications for postgraduate study. Speak directly to the institution for further details of how and when to apply.

Preparing a research proposal

The **research proposal** forms a vital component of any application to a research-based course; it should explain the nature of your research and how you will carry it out. An effective research proposal helps the institution to decide whether the work is feasible and original and whether they can offer you supervision – all determining factors when deciding whether to accept an applicant. Careful research into whether an institution has the strengths that match your area of interest can reduce rejections; make sure you talk to the department before submitting any proposal.

The proposal is a chance to sell yourself and to stand out from fellow applicants in a competitive market place. As with an effective personal statement, it should be focused, clear and concise. Different universities and departments specify different word counts, ranging between 500 and a few thousand words. The proposal should explain the project and its importance, setting out how the work will be completed and its scale. Your university department will be able to provide further advice on this process.

After application

After you send off your application, it is then a case of sitting back and waiting patiently. This part of the process can seem to last forever. If you have applied online, you may be able to track your progress online too, rather than waiting for the post to arrive. UCAS, UKPASS and GTTR enable online tracking, allowing you to receive and respond to offers securely online.

Interview

Some courses and some institutions will require you to attend
an interview before they consider making an offer. If you are
in the UK or are able to travel to the UK for interview, this will
be part of the process to determine whether you are offered a
place. For those requiring a visitor visa to enter the country,
you will be provided with the documentation to apply for a visa.
However, timescales are often very tight and alternative ways of
interviewing may be preferable. Some universities will interview
in your home country, over the telephone or through Skype.

Offers

If the university believes you to be a suitable candidate, they will
make you an offer. If you have already completed your previous
studies, this is likely to be an **unconditional offer**. If not, they
will give you certain conditions to meet in order to gain your
place. This may mean you have to achieve a certain grade in the
IELTS exam, your high school studies or your degree.

Once all your offers have been received, the UCAS system allows
you to accept one firm choice and to select an insurance choice
(normally requiring lower grades) as a back-up option. If all
of your choices have been unsuccessful, there are facilities
including UCAS Extra and Clearing (see www.ucas.com) where
you will have the chance to make additional choices.

Postgraduate systems like GTTR and UKPASS do not offer the
option to make an insurance choice and only allow respondents
to accept or decline a place.

Where you have applied directly to one or more institutions,
there is no formal process for accepting and declining other than

by writing directly to the institution. It is probably not advisable to keep outstanding offers from too many institutions.

Confirmation of Acceptance for Studies

If you need a visa or entry clearance and your institution is a Highly Trusted Sponsor, they will be able to issue you with the **Confirmation of Acceptance for Studies (CAS)** number that you need in order to apply for these documents. See Chapter 3, 'Getting ready to research', for further details on Highly Trusted Sponsors (see p.39). For new students, the CAS is generally issued once all conditions of the offer have been met and the institution has been accepted as a firm choice.

Normally, your institution will need to receive the following before issuing the CAS:

- a copy of a valid passport
- the results of any examinations
- the results of English language testing
- a deposit.

The CAS is valid for six months, and new students can submit a visa application up to three months before the commencement of studies. Do not apply any earlier than this, as your application will be refused.

Next steps

Receiving your offer (and your CAS) is your first step on the road to studying in the UK; once you have this you can start the process of applying for a visa or entry clearance. Other key tasks involve looking for accommodation and finalising the funding for your studies, which we will look at in the next chapter.

University of Sunderland

Innovate. Create. Graduate.

The Faculty of Business and Law at the University of Sunderland is recognised worldwide. With students from over 70 countries and a presence on three continents, the faculty is playing a major part in preparing tomorrow's leaders for success.

The faculty is home to three academic departments, with each of these providing an insight into the workings of some of the key areas and industries of modern society, an insight which will one day propel you into a successful and fulfilling career.

Sunderland Business School has a reputation for delivering programmes influenced by the latest business and management thinking. Industrial placements and degree courses covering a range of business functions ensure that as a graduate you are equipped with the knowledge and skills needed to find employment or set up your own business. Because of this, it is easy to see why Sunderland Business School is currently Number 1 in the North East of England (The Guardian University Guide, 2012)

The Department of Law has an excellent reputation for student satisfaction (The Guardian University Guide, 2012) and is renowned for its open-door policy and the level of support it offers. Because the department allows you to tailor your law degree to suit your personal interests and continue pursuing specific legal areas at postgraduate level, its courses now also have growing international popularity.

The Department of Tourism, Hospitality and Events has a strong research pedigree, with research at Sunderland ranked as world-leading. Fieldtrips and industrial placements across the globe provide you with an applied understanding of tourism, while a dedicated teaching team are on hand to impart both their academic and practical experience.

Whatever your future ambitions, make a life-changing decision by coming to study at The Faculty of Business and Law at the University of Sunderland.

Case study

Song Cheng, International Student

Travelling away from home and coming somewhere so different was daunting at first. I left my family and friends behind and came to study for a degree in England. I didn't know much about Sunderland but was drawn to the Tourism department, which has an excellent reputation, both in the UK and beyond. I had read that Sunderland was a scenic city by the sea, and I was keen to see this for myself.

From the first day of my studies I felt like I had found my new home. The course I enrolled on was challenging, but this gave me the perfect opportunity to develop my critical thinking skills and research into a range of areas. The teaching staff really supported me throughout my degree, and were always happy to provide me with advice and share their experiences. The fact that they were so approachable meant that I could discuss topics on an informal level, and pick up information without even realising it.

Sunderland is an inexpensive, compact city with everything you need on your doorstep. Travelling from one campus to another only takes a few minutes so you have a wealth of resources at your disposal. The university facilities are first-class, and show why students choose to study here from all over the world. The first time I came to the Sir Tom Cowie Campus at St Peter's, where my course is taught, I knew that I had made the right choice.

From my time at the University of Sunderland I have been able to gain my independence and experience being immersed in another culture. Coming here was a once-in-a-lifetime opportunity and I have enjoyed my time here so much that I have now enrolled onto a postgraduate programme.

Chapter 7
Fees and funding

One of the first questions a potential student is likely to ask is: "How much are the fees?" The second question might well be: "Can I get any financial support?" In this chapter, you will get an idea of the fees you will have to pay and find out about sources of financial support.

Categories for overseas students

Much of this book, and the information relating to study in the UK, divides overseas students into several categories. You need to know which category you fall into, as the fees you will be expected to pay at public institutions, and any support that you may be entitled to, are dependent on the type of student you are considered to be: home, EU or international. It is worth noting that many private institutions charge the same fees, regardless of status.

The rules determining whether you are classed as a home, EU or international student can be complex. The rules differ slightly between all four UK nations, but most notably between Scotland and the rest of the UK. The details provided here are a brief and basic overview of information; they are not a definitive list of criteria. **UKCISA** has a useful information sheet on tuition fees at www.ukcisa.org.uk. Complex cases should be discussed in more detail with your institution. If you feel your institution may have assessed you incorrectly, you can contact your institution's students' union or UKCISA.

Categories for non-EU nationals

If you are a non-EU or non-EEA (European Economic Area) national who has been living outside the EEA within the last three years, then you are likely to be classed as an international student. If you are a non-EU national who has settled in the UK and has been resident there for the last three years (although not for the purposes of full-time education) then you may be considered a home student. You should check your status as soon as possible.

Non-EU nationals aged 16 to 18, accompanying their parents who are legally in the UK, should be classed as home students for fees purposes, so will not have to pay fees if attending publicly funded further education establishments.

Non-EU nationals who are married to (or in a civil partnership with) a UK national will pay home student fees as long as they have been married and resident in the UK for a year by the relevant date (see text box below). Non-EU nationals who are married to (or the civil partner or child of) an EU national will only pay home fees if they have been ordinarily resident in the EEA for three years by the relevant date.

Relevant dates

England, Wales and Northern Ireland

Any requirements for residence purposes must be met by the relevant date. For courses starting between 1 August and 31 December, the relevant date is 1 September: so, for a student who is starting a course in the autumn to be classed as an EU student, they should have been living within the

EEA for three years by 1 September. For courses that
start between 1 January and 31 March, the relevant date
is 1 January. For courses that start between 1 April and
30 June, the relevant date is 1 April, while courses
starting between 1 and 31 July have a relevant date
of 1 July.

Scotland

The relevant date for Scotland is 1 August for courses
starting between 1 August and 31 December. 1 January is
used for courses starting between 1 January and 31 March,
1 April for courses starting between 1 April and 30 June,
and 1 July for courses starting in the month of July.

Categories for EU nationals

If you are an EU or EEA national who has been settled and
resident in the EEA (but outside the UK) for the last three
years, then you will be classed as an EU student; you will pay
the same fees as a UK national, but will not be entitled to all
the same sources of financial support. If you have been living
outside the EEA in the last three years, you will be classed as an
international student, unless you can show that your absence
was temporary.

EU nationals settled and ordinarily resident in the UK for the
past three years can apply for support with tuition fees and living
costs. EEA and Swiss nationals who are in the UK as migrant
workers or are classed as self-employed can also apply for support
with tuition fees and living expenses, such as maintenance loans
and grants; if you fit into this category, you do not need to meet
the three-year residency requirement. Special requirements apply
to children of Turkish workers. You can find out more at www.
ukcisa.org.uk/student/fees_student_support.php.

A registration certificate is not a mandatory requirement for EU students studying in the UK, but it might be useful to have one, as it gives proof of your right to live and work in the UK. UKBA provides information on why and how to apply at www.ukba. homeoffice.uk/eucitizens/documents-eea-national.

Countries of the EU

Austria, Belgium, Bulgaria, Republic of Cyprus, Czech Republic, Denmark, Estonia, Finland, France, Germany, Greece, Hungary, Ireland, Italy, Latvia, Lithuania, Luxembourg, Malta, Netherlands, Poland, Portugal, Romania, Slovakia, Slovenia, Spain, Sweden and the UK.

Countries of the EEA

The EEA is made up of all the countries in the EU plus Iceland, Liechtenstein and Norway. Although not within the EEA, nationals of Switzerland have the same rights as EEA nationals (for funding purposes).

Fees and funding for international students

This section is for those students who fall into the international student category; separate rules apply to those classed as home or EU students (see p.111).

International students are charged fees to cover the full cost of their tuition, regardless of the level of study. This includes the cost of lectures, seminars and tutorials, but also means you will benefit from the libraries and research facilities, computers, laboratories and workshops. You will have the opportunity to work with respected thinkers and leaders in their field, along with the support of tutors and a range of support services. All of this is provided in a setting where your independent thinking skills will be able to flourish.

Some **higher education institutions** offer a fixed-fee scheme, whereby students on courses of over a year pay the same fee for each year of their programme. This helps you to plan financially and budget appropriately. You will need to check whether your university offers this system.

In addition to course fees, you will find that you may be expected to pay for college fees, books and materials, equipment, field trips and your graduation. Postgraduate students may be expected to pay research support fees or bench fees. Ask your university about any extra costs before you commit to a course of study. Understanding the full expenses for each university you are interested in should help you to make a realistic comparison on a cost-by-cost basis.

Further education fees for international students

Courses within a further education setting are also known as career-based or pre-university courses. Somewhat confusingly, some pre-university courses can be taken in a university setting.

The fees for further education vary widely. According to figures provided by the British Council, average course fees per year are as follows:

- AS and A levels   £4,000 to £17,000
- BTECs and other vocational courses   £4,000 to £6,000
- HNCs/HNDs   £5,000 to £10,000
- Foundation degrees   £7,000 to £12,000
- International Foundation courses   £4,000 to £17,000

Undergraduate fees for international students

Fees charged to international students vary from around £8,000 per year to more than £20,000. Laboratory and workshop-based courses, for example science or clinical studies, tend to have higher running costs and therefore higher fees.

Universities UK carries out an annual survey into university fees for international students: the organisation asks higher education providers to supply information on the fees they charge. The median results for undergraduate courses in the 2011/2012 survey are as follows:

- classroom-based courses: £10,500 (up £700 on the previous year)
- lab or workshop-based courses: £12,800 (up £800 on last year)
- clinical medicine or dentistry courses: £25,600–£25,700

Postgraduate fees for international students

Fees for postgraduate students range widely, from around £9,000 for a classroom-based research course to £30,000 or more for the most expensive MBA (classroom-based) course, according to the British Council. As with undergraduate study, laboratory and workshop-based courses tend to attract higher fees, with clinical courses coming at the very top. Taught courses tend to attract slightly higher fees than those that are research-based. The wide range of fees for MBAs can be linked to a department's prestige, ranking, networking opportunities or increased earning potential. See www.ft.com/businesseducation/mba for global rankings.

The Universities UK 2011/2012 survey into tuition fees provides the following median figures for postgraduate courses:

- taught classroom-based courses: £11,100 (up £900 on last year)

- taught lab or workshop-based courses: £13,100 (an increase of £500 on last year)
- taught clinical medicine or dentistry courses: £23,400 to £27,000
- research classroom-based course: £10,600 (up £400 on the previous year)
- research lab or workshop-based courses: £13,000 (a £200 increase)
- research clinical medicine or dentistry courses: £26,600 to £26,700
- classroom-based MBAs: £15,600 (up £2,100 on last year).

You can view the full survey of international student fees at the Universities UK website, www.universitiesuk.ac.uk.

Part-time study for international students

Most international students requiring a student (**Tier 4**) visa will not be eligible to study a part-time course. In certain cases, part-time study can be permitted: if, for example, a student from overseas does not require a student visa because of their circumstances, or if a full-time student with a relevant visa chooses to do some part-time or short courses to supplement their studies. There are strict rules about the circumstances that enable part-time study. You are advised to discuss the matter further with your institution. Part-time fees are generally a proportion of the full-time costs.

Student financial support for international students

International students are expected to fund the full costs of their studies and all associated costs. There is no financial support available through the channels open to home or EU students. Consequently, some courses are not accessible to international students. For example, nursing and midwifery courses require students to be eligible for an **NHS**-funded bursary. International students cannot get the bursary, so cannot apply for the courses. Some universities offer alternative options specifically aimed at international students.

It is always worth checking in your home country whether any assistance with funding can be transferred to your studies in the UK. Some countries allow the transfer of student loans if studying abroad.

Scholarships for international students

There are a range of scholarships available for undergraduate and postgraduate taught and research-based programmes. Most are highly competitive, awarded often on the basis of academic excellence. Some scholarships are offered to students in particular circumstances, or to those who are studying or researching particular subjects. It is important to note that most scholarships only partially cover the costs of study, so you will need to supplement them with other means.

It is not easy to get a scholarship; there are far more applicants than awards, so many applicants end up disappointed. The research and the application process can be time-consuming. You will need to research fully your options around funding your course in the UK. Since the majority of applicants are unsuccessful, consider how you will support yourself financially if you don't get a scholarship.

Some international students fall victim to fraudsters in their quest for a scholarship. Genuine organisations will not send you unsolicited emails asking for personal information, financial details or money. You should not have to pay to search or apply for a scholarship.

Far more scholarships are available for postgraduate research-based degrees than for taught postgraduate or undergraduate study. There may be very specific criteria in order to meet a particular scholarship's requirements. You will need to start researching and applying for scholarships early; some deadlines may close one academic year beforehand, so you'll need to start your preparations at least 18 months in advance.

A first step in finding out about scholarships is to approach your own government's education department to see if they offer any support to study abroad. The next port of call should be the **British Council** (or embassy or high commission) in your home country. Education UK (www.educationuk.org) has a web-based scholarship search covering some of the national scholarship schemes. You can also search for details on your institution's website and approach your own department; they tend to offer a range of more specific schemes relating to the university or the course of study.

Nadya Pramudita of Indonesia gained a scholarship to study for a pre-university diploma at the United World College (UWC) of the Atlantic in Wales. The college has 350 students aged 16 to 19 from all over the world. She describes the application process.

66 First I filled in an application that consisted of personal achievements, school records, an essay and the application form itself. They gave me a phone call after a few weeks saying that I was accepted into the next round. Then I met them, along with the other 11 finalists, for an interview day including a personal interview and a group discussion. After a week or so, they gave the results and now I am here. I think the whole process took me approximately two months, including the time needed to collect all the documents. **99**

Nadya Pramudita

Here is a selection of some of the scholarships available.

- Commonwealth Scholarship and Fellowship Plan
  For study at undergraduate level and upwards for
  applicants from certain Commonwealth countries.
  www.csfp-online.org
- Chevening Scholarships
  A highly prestigious award for postgraduate students
  planning to return to their home country and
  contribute to its development.
  www.facebook.com/officialchevening
- Marshall Scholarships
  Aimed at high-preforming US citizens for postgraduate
  study in the UK.
  www.marshallscholarship.org
- 9/11 Scholarships
  Awarded to children or dependants of victims of the
  11 September attacks on the US, or of other subsequent
  terrorist tragedies, for study at further education,
  undergraduate or postgraduate level in the UK.
  www.britishcouncil.org/911scholarships.htm
- Fulbright Awards Programme
  A range of different study awards for US citizens
  mainly at postgraduate level. The Summer Institutes
  offer undergraduate students the chance to experience
  an academic and cultural summer programme.
  www.fulbright.co.uk
- Newton International Fellowships
  Awarded to post-doctoral researchers in physical,
  natural and social sciences and the humanities.
  www.newtonfellowships.org
- Gates Cambridge Scholarships
  Awarded to outstanding students from outside the
  UK for postgraduate study in any discipline at the

University of Cambridge.

www.gatesscholar.org

- Mitchell Scholars Program

  This award seeks applications from US citizens aged
  18 to 30 for one year's postgraduate study in the
  Republic of Ireland or Northern Ireland.

  www.us-irelandalliance.org

- Rhodes Scholarships

  Two-year full scholarships for postgraduate study at
  the University of Oxford, for applicants from a range of
  countries.

  www.rhodeshouse.ox.ac.uk

- Saltire Scholarships

  Funding towards a master's programme in a 'priority'
  subject at any Scottish university. Applications are
  welcomed from applicants from Canada, China, India
  and the US.

  www.talentscotland.com/students/study/scholarships/
  saltire-scholarships.aspx

Many more schemes operate through a range of organisations
including UNESCO, the World Health Organization and the
European Commission.

Remember to:

- plan ahead
- start the research early
- explore the options in your home country initially
- apply in good time
- make sure you meet the selection criteria
- follow the application procedures to the letter.

Do your research and don't underestimate the cost of living and studying. **99**

Alexa Johnson, US

Other sources of funding for international students

A range of charities and trusts, small and large, offer funding in varying amounts. Each has its own eligibility criteria, deadlines and application procedures.

Speak to your home country education department initially. If you are already in the UK, approach your university, which should have a copy of the **Grants Register**, a worldwide guide to postgraduate funding.

There may be some opportunities to earn small amounts of money at university when studying at postgraduate level; consider graduate teaching, research assistantships, academic support or hall tutorships.

International students may fund their studies using a combination of sources, from private finance to sponsorship and scholarships. The key message is to arrange funding before you come to the UK.

Financial or government sponsorship for international students

If you are lucky enough to secure financial sponsorship from your home government, the UK government, the British Council, an international organisation, an international company or a university, then you are classed as having an official financial sponsor. You can use this as evidence for your visa that you have enough money to pay fees and living expenses. Any shortfalls in funding provided by the financial sponsor will have to be evidenced by you. See Chapter 8 on visas (see p.125) for details of how to apply.

Fees and funding for EU students

For fees purposes, EU students are treated the same as home students; however, there are key differences in the financial support that might be available for study.

Support for the costs of studying is available to EU students in certain cases. Sometimes EU students will be exempt from paying fees. Support may also come in the form of a repayable loan or a non-repayable grant. It is important to understand the type of support you are getting. If you need to repay the money, you must be clear about what the interest rate will be, how much you will have to repay and when you will have to do so.

Certain EU countries offer portability in funding for studies. It is worth asking in your home country whether any funding you are entitled to at home can be transferred to your studies in the UK.

Further education fees for EU students

EU students will be charged at the same rate as home students. Fees vary according to the college and the country where you choose to study, although students aged 16 to 18 should not be charged fees. Some full-time courses and specific part-time courses do not have fees. Most full-time further education students in Scotland receive a fee waiver.

Where fees are payable, the price of full-time courses varies widely,with some colleges charging around £250 and others up to £2,000 per year. Part-time courses tend to range from around £100 to £1,000 per year.

Student financial support for EU further education students

You may be exempt from paying full fees if one of the following conditions applies:

- you are under 19
- you are in receipt of specific means-tested benefits
- you are on a low income
- you have a disability.

Financial support for the costs associated with study may be available to EU and home students studying in further education. This is known as Discretionary Learner Support and is administered through your college. Specific conditions apply to this funding, so you should discuss it directly with your college.

Additional support may be available for those who meet the UK residency requirements, including a fee waiver if you are studying your first course at level 2 or 3 (and meet certain requirements). Ask your college for further details of whether you may be eligible. Professional and Career Development Loans are another option to consider. Find out more at www.direct.gov.uk (search for 'career development loans').

Changes to further education support

From autumn 2013, further education support in England looks set to change, with the introduction of a new system of FE loans. Based on current information, this system will be open to students aged 24 and over who are studying courses at level 3 or 4. It looks like EU students will need to have three years' UK residence.

new college nottingham

**Excellence
Employability
Enterprise**

Study in Nottingham

Study:
Further Education
A-Levels
Foundation Programmes
University-level Courses
English Language

New College Nottingham is one of the largest
colleges in the UK, offering an exciting range of
study programmes. Based centrally, Nottingham
is a major student destination for students from
around the world. Find out what we have to offer

Contact the International Team at New College Nottingham:

Telephone: +44 (0) 115 9104610 / 9104615 / 9104668

Email: international@ncn.ac.uk

www.ncn.ac.uk

Greetings from
Gower College Swansea

Gower College Swansea
Coleg Gŵyr Abertawe

- Over 45 A Level subjects
- HNC/HND courses
- Pre-University Foundation programmes
- English Language courses
- Oxbridge Preparation programme
- Vocational programmes

- Very competitive fees
- Located in one of the safest cities in the UK
- September and January start dates
- Individual support for International students
- 98% A Level pass rate

UKBA
Highly
Trusted
Sponsor

International Office,
Gower College Swansea,
Tycoch, Swansea, Wales,
United Kingdom. SA2 9EB

0044 (0)1792 201290/890707
international@gowercollegeswansea.ac.uk
www.gowercollegeswansea.ac.uk
facebook Gower College Swansea International

WESTMINSTER BUSINESS SCHOOL

YOU CAN PUT OUR SPECIALISED MASTERS STRAIGHT TO WORK FOR YOU

Taught by academics with extensive business experience, our wide rage of specialist postgraduate degrees can be applied immediately in the real world of work.

Add value to your career by discovering more about the

wide range of courses available at one of the biggest business schools based in the heart of London.

To find out more about our excellent masters programmes please visit

WESTMINSTER.AC.UK/WBS

UNIVERSITY OF
VISION
STRATEGY
OPPORTUNITY
WESTMINSTER ⌗

EFMD

EQUIS
ACCREDITED

Accredited by
Association
of MBAs

Business School

Join our global business community

Take control of your future with a postgraduate degree at Newcastle University Business School

For more information on our diverse range of programmes visit:
www.ncl.ac.uk/nubs

You can find us on:

A new perspective on
business education

The Business School is one of the largest, most diverse schools in Newcastle University, with 2,800 students from over 80 countries. Part of the UK's elite Russell Group, we are a research-intensive institution, delivering programmes of the highest quality and one of only 128 business schools, worldwide, to receive accreditation from the European agency EFMD under its EQUIS scheme. We offer undergraduate, postgraduate and research programmes, many of which are accredited by professional bodies.

Relevant programmes

All our programmes are designed with the global business community in mind and students are encouraged to think entrepreneurially. Our research expertise is focused on influencing current business policy and practice – as well as core aspects of management, we specialise in knowledge, innovation, technology, and enterprise through our dedicated KITE research centre, which is currently developing its research in the field of entrepreneurship.

For more information on our diverse range of programmes visit: **www.ncl.ac.uk/nubs**

Challenging education

The School strives to create the best environment for high-calibre students and faculty to be intellectually challenged and rewarded. Our new £50m building hosts networking spaces where students and staff collaborate. Our professional accreditations ensure we take a critical approach to the relevance of our teaching, and we are committed to recruiting the best minds in business to our academic faculty. It is challenging, but the School seeks to attract students who share our view, that active participation in learning and engagement develop the skills to make a real difference in the business world.

Vibrant city-centre location

Newcastle has twice been voted the best university city in the UK. It is renowned for its architectural beauty, cultural scene and lively nightlife, as well as its friendliness. Surrounded by some of the UK's most unspoilt countryside and coastline, Newcastle also offers excellent value for money, making it an affordable destination for students of all backgrounds.

'Newcastle remains a destination for the savvy student, seeking a high-quality top 20 university experience in a buzzing city, where the student pound goes appreciably further than in other parts of Britain.'
**The Sunday Times
Good University Guide 2012**

Dual Award programmes

Truly global business management today requires the ability to challenge norms, adopt new perspectives, and balance the values and needs of a wide and diverse audience.

The Business School has developed a series of programmes that take students into other regions of the world, to study, exchange ideas, and apply cutting-edge theory to practice. At postgraduate level we offer the Dual Award in Advanced International Business Management and the Dual Award in Operations Management, both run jointly with The University of Groningen in the Netherlands.

Careers

The University's Careers Service is award-winning, and the Business School focuses on student employability through international internships, placements and the support of a dedicated careers advisor.

The Business School's graduate employment rates are well above the national average: in 2010, 96 per cent of employment-seeking graduates secured jobs within six months.

Student profile: Julius Nierwetberg
Strategic Planning and Investment MSc

'The Master of Science in Strategic Planning and Investment appeared to be an excellent theoretical supplement to my internship in the strategic planning department of a German car producer, especially with regard to valuable analytical skills. The quality of teaching was important to me – it is very high at Newcastle University, ranking amongst the top 20 universities in the UK. I consider the University's connections to major multinational companies very important in an increasingly globalising world; in fact, I made my first contact with my future employer there. I was also attracted by the beautiful city of Newcastle upon Tyne and the international student body. All in all, my expectations were exceeded in every respect.'

UWC ATLANTIC COLLEGE

Transformative and Challenging Education

A UWC Atlantic College education is the beginning of a life-changing journey. Based in a 12th Century castle on the coast of South Wales, United Kingdom, a truly diverse international student body studies for the IB Diploma and learns to respect difference.

Through community projects our students demonstrate their commitment to making a positive difference in the world.

Celebrating 50 years
of pioneering international education

Find out more about the opportunities available for
16 -19 year olds by visiting **www.atlanticcollege.org**

Innovate. Create.
Graduate. Faculty of Business and Law at the University of Sunderland

High quality undergraduate and postgraduate programmes in:
Business • Law • Tourism • Events Management

No. 1 Business School in the North East of England (The Guardian University Guide 2012)

£2 OFF*

ALL STUDENT ESSENTIALS

These practical and jargon-free guides show students how to easily master essential study skills in just one hour, covering every key area, from developing critical thinking and essay writing to revision and exam know-how.

STUDENT ESSENTIALS

IN 1 HOUR

ESSAY WRITING

Sophie Fuggle

£2 OFF
ONLY £5.99 ~~RRP £7.99~~
Available to buy at
www.**trotman**.co.uk
Enter STUDENT at the checkout

STUDENT ESSENTIALS

Undergraduate fees for EU students

The fees for undergraduate-level study vary according to the UK country where you choose to study.

England

In September 2012, a new system of funding was introduced in England; this has resulted in English universities charging tution fees of between £6,000 and £9,000 per year. Many universities have opted for fees at or near the highest rate of £9,000. Some colleges of further education offering university-level qualifications may charge less than £6,000.

The maximum level for fees will remain at £9,000 for new students starting university in the 2013/2014 academic year.

Scotland

EU students studying in Scotland do not normally have to pay fees but must apply through the Student Awards Agency for Scotland (SAAS).

Northern Ireland

If you are studying in Northern Ireland, you will be charged fees of £3,465 in September 2012.

Wales

Although the fees in Wales have increased to £6,000 to £9,000 per year from autumn 2012, EU students will not be expected to pay the full amount. Non-UK EU students will receive a fee grant from the Welsh Assembly Government to cover any tuition fee costs over £3,465 in 2012–13.

Fees for a 'sandwich' (or work placement) year are likely to be a proportion of the full tuition fees payable in the country and institution you choose.

Student financial support for EU undergraduate students

If you are studying in England, Wales or Northern Ireland at undergraduate level, you can take out a student loan up to the full amount of your tuition fees: £9,000 in England and £3,465 in Wales and Northern Ireland. Loans have to be repaid from the April after you finish the course and when you are earning over a set amount (£21,000 per year if you study in England and Wales and £15,795 if you study in Northern Ireland).

EU undergraduate students in Scotland do not have to pay fees.

Previous study at degree level will affect your chances of applying for funding (with the exception of courses in medicine, dentistry, veterinary science, architecture and social work). In England, Wales and Northern Ireland, previous degree-level study (even if you received no funding for it from the UK) will have an impact on your chance to gain funding for tuition fees. In Scotland, this ruling applies if you have received any support from EU funds for previous study.

EU students are not eligible to take out loans for living costs unless they meet the UK three-year residence rule or they originally came to the UK as a migrant worker.

For further information, if you will be studying in England, go to www.direct.gov.uk. If you will be studying in Scotland, go to www.saas.gov.uk. For Wales visit www.studentfinancewales. co.uk, and if you will be studying in Northern Ireland go to www.nidirect.gov.uk.

Postgraduate fees for EU students

Postgraduate fees for EU students are the same as for home students, currently ranging from £3,400 and upwards per year, although some course fees can be considerably higher. As with international fees, taught courses or laboratory-based courses tend to be the most expensive. MBAs tend to top the price list with some institutions charging in excess of £30,000.

Times Higher Education suggests that the average UK postgraduate fee for home and EU students in 2011/2012 was £6,184.

Student financial support for EU postgraduate students

England, Wales and Northern Ireland

Student loans and similar support are not normally available for postgraduate study in England, Wales and Northern Ireland. Slightly different rules apply to courses such as teaching, social work and NHS-funded courses. Funding for study at postgraduate level normally has to come through other sources including scholarships, private funding and sponsorship.

Scotland

Tuition fees loans are available to home or EU students for certain professional or vocational postgraduate diploma level courses. See the SAAS website for lists of funded courses. You can apply through SAAS for loans of up to £3,400 for full time study or £1,700 for part time study. You will be expected to start repaying your loan once you have finished the course and are earning over £15,795 per year.

Part-time fees for EU students

EU students can also study part-time in the UK. Fees for part-time courses will normally be a proportion of the normal full-time equivalent.

Student financial support for part-time EU undergraduate students

If you are studying a part-time undergraduate course at a university in Scotland, Wales or Northern Ireland, you can apply for a non-repayable grant to help with your tuition fees. The amount that you will be entitled to depends on your personal circumstances, your household income, the intensity of your course and the country where you choose to study. In Scotland, only those students with three years' residency in the UK and settled status in Scotland are eligible to apply for the grant of up to £500. The maximum grant available in Wales is £1,000 and in Northern Ireland it is £1,230. Find out more about support for part-time study at the student finance website of your country of study:

- www.saas.gov.uk for Scotland
- www.studentfinancewales.co.uk for Wales
- www.nidirect.gov.uk for Northern Ireland.

For those studying part-time in England, a tuition fee loan is available of up to £6,750; repayment of the loan will start from the April after you complete your course and once you are earning over £21,000 per year.

Scholarships for EU students

There is a range of scholarships open to EU students. As is the case for international students, the process is highly competitive, most awards are for postgraduate study and many awards do not cover the full costs of study. Remember: most students are not successful in gaining any form of scholarship and only a tiny minority are fully funded in their studies.

EU students can be considered for scholarships or studentships issued by the seven Research Councils in the UK. EU nationals may qualify for fees-only awards, but they would not be considered for a stipend, which is for living costs. The Research Council awards cover taught and research-based programmes.

- Arts and Humanities Research Council
- Biotechnology and Biological Sciences Research Council
- Economic and Social Research Council
- Engineering and Physical Sciences Research Council
- Medical Research Council
- Natural Environment Research Council
- Science and Technology Facilities Council

You can get further information and links to each Research Council website at www.rcuk.ac.uk. Any applications for scholarships should be made through your institution.

See the section on scholarships for international students for some tips on applying for scholarships (see p.106). Remember to search in your home country initially. You should approach your institution about specific awards relating to your area of study or institution. You can use the following websites to start searching for opportunities:

- www.educationuk.org
- www.scholarship-search.org.uk
- www.prospects.ac.uk/funding.

Other sources of funding for EU students

A large number of charities, trusts and foundations offer awards to support students in their studies. The awards and the institutions vary; each one has its own requirements, applications and deadlines.

Speak to your home country education department first. If you are in the UK, you could ask your institution if they have a copy of the Grants Register, a worldwide guide to postgraduate funding. They can also help you gain information through **EGAS** (the Educational Grants Advisory Service).

Funding for students with disabilities

Under the UK Equality Act 2010, a person has a disability if:

a. they have a physical or mental impairment, and
b. the impairment has a substantial and long-term adverse effect on their ability to carry out normal day-to-day activities.

Within the UK, disability includes specific learning difficulties such as dyslexia, long-term illnesses and mental health conditions.

Extra funding is not available from the UK government to pay for the costs of supporting EU and international students with a disability. However, the Equality Act 2010 states that it is illegal for someone to be discriminated against on the basis of their disability. Colleges and universities should make reasonable adjustments to help you with your disability-related needs. This might include a note-taker, additional time in exams or materials in alternative formats. More expensive support may be dependent on funding.

You are advised to make early contact with your institution to discuss how you will be supported. Ask how you can make contact with the college or university disability co-ordinator or learning support co-ordinator. Your university will be able to advise you further or work with you to investigate sources of funding, such as:

- sponsors
- scholarships

- support from your own government
- non-governmental organisations in your home country.

The Higher Education Accessibility Guide (HEAG) provides information on disability support services at UK and EU universities at www.european-agency.org/agency-projects/ heag. Disability Rights UK may also be able to provide some information at www.disabilityrights.uk.org/disabledstudents.htm.

STUDENT CASE STUDY
David Stoll, Luxembourg

David Stoll, an EU student from Erpeldange in Luxembourg, seems to be enjoying his education at the University of Aberdeen in Scotland. "I have been having a great time, which is one of the reasons I am now doing my third degree in the UK." He explains how he found out about study in the UK and how he adjusted to student life in a new country.

"I always wanted to study in an English-speaking country and I heard good things about UK universities." David took the opportunity to attend an event in his home country to get started with researching institutions. "I went to a universities and higher education fair in Luxembourg City, as well as doing intensive research on the internet and ordering a number of university prospectuses."

He used the information on degree courses he had gathered in person, online and in prospectuses and compared them to his interests in history, international relations and politics. David narrowed his choices down to a handful, ready to complete his UCAS application.

"As everything was done through UCAS, it was a fairly straightforward application process and I did not encounter any problems. Applying for my postgraduate studies was even easier as it was handled directly by the university in question."

As an EU student studying in Scotland, David enjoyed the benefit of free tuition fees for undergraduate study. "For my undergraduate degree I applied to SAAS [Student Awards Agency for Scotland] for funding and they paid my tuition fees for me. My government sponsored me for my postgraduate degrees.

Generally, tuition fees and the cost of living are higher than in Luxembourg, but well worth it."

David describes moving to Scotland as "rather smooth and painless". Before he arrived in the UK, he was bombarded with leaflets and information to aid the process. When he arrived in Aberdeen, the support continued. "There were current students welcoming new students at the airport and there were lots of events during **freshers' week** helping new students get to know the campus and the city. I also got to meet with my adviser of studies, who was there to help with any academic questions and problems."

David describes the UK as "multicultural and diverse". He hasn't really had any difficulties adjusting to the language here. "It took a little bit of time getting used to all the various English idioms and expressions and to understand all the pop culture references, but I would hardly call this a difficulty. Some British accents take some getting used to."

It hasn't been a huge leap for him educationally. "As far as I can tell, there are not that many differences between education in Luxembourg and in the UK. It is the same mix between attending lectures, doing independent study and participating in tutorials and seminars."

David recommends choosing wisely between all the options. "Make an informed decision about what degree and what university to go for. Get as much information as possible. Don't be afraid to contact universities directly and ask for extra information. If possible, go and attend an open day or arrange a private visit."

David originally applied for university accommodation but encountered an unusual problem. David is 6 feet 8 inches (2.03m) tall and the bed was too short for him, so he had to look elsewhere. "I easily found private accommodation with the help of

the Students' Association. Thankfully, I found a friendly landlord
who lengthened my bed for me.

"I had heard a lot of rumours about British cooking, but most
of them turned out not to be true. Thanks to the Commonwealth
there are a lot of different restaurants and cuisines available.
Though it's still hard finding proper European-style bread.

"Living costs in the UK can be rather high, but a lot of shops,
restaurants and cinemas in the big university towns offer great
student discounts and cheap shopping. It is always good to have
your student ID card on you 24/7.

"Travel in the UK and Europe can be a bit expensive. It's always
best to book well in advance and to look around for special
student offers."

David found it easy to find a part-time job and ended up working
at the university.

He has taken advantage of the range of extra-curricular
opportunities, getting involved with various clubs and societies.
"Becoming a member of about a dozen societies has expanded my
horizons and allowed me to take part in many fun events."

He has made lifelong friends during his time in the UK. "From
my own experience, the best things about studying here are the
open and friendly environment and the many awesome friends I
made during my years here. Some have now moved on to other
universities or have got jobs, but we are still in contact and meet
up whenever possible."

Westminster Business School

WESTMINSTER BUSINESS SCHOOL
UNIVERSITY OF WESTMINSTER

Westminster Business School, located in the heart of London, is one of the largest centres for business and management education in the UK. The school offers a number of specialist business master's courses, both recognised and accredited by a number of professional bodies.

The school is also engaged in conducting applied research that is relevant to all areas of business, and much of which has gained an international reputation. Finally, we have built a reputation for enterprise, knowledge transfer in the London region and work with public and private organisations across the UK.

We are London's leading professionally focused and research-engaged business school.

The school is cosmopolitan, having a diverse student population which reflects London's demographic variety and nearly a third of our full-time students come from outside the UK.

Our staff are also drawn from many countries, and every year we welcome visiting scholars and researchers from all over the world. Although we are a school with a strongly international outlook, we also draw on a long tradition of providing part-time courses for Londoners. For nearly 80 years the school has served the needs of busy professionals and business people living or working in the capital giving our full-time students a unique opportunity to network with active business community.

Our strong links with the London business circle and government enable us to bring practitioners and headline-makers into the classroom on a regular basis. In turn we help arrange student placements, internships and mentoring which give our students an important hands-on experience and involvement with the world of work.

The school has growing research and consultancy strengths in a range of areas, including employment research, financial services and international finance, leadership, and business strategy. We host conferences, workshops, seminars and other events open to the public, and regard the dissemination of new ideas to the outside world as an important part of our mission.

We offer master's in the following areas:

- MBA
- Business and Management
- Accounting, Finance and Economics
- Marketing
- Human Resource Management
- Business Information Management and Operations

www.westminster.ac.uk/wbs

Chapter 8
Visas

Applying for the correct permission to come and study in the UK can be a daunting and confusing business. Give yourself time to get to grips with what is needed and when. You will probably come across a lot of conflicting information online; a lot of the opinion provided on discussion boards can be subjective and is often plain wrong. You do not need to rely on the opinion of people who are not experts in this field. The UK has a regulation scheme through the **OISC** (Office of the Immigration Services Commissioner) for anyone providing immigration advice or services. Many educational institutions dealing with international students have staff advising at OISC level 1 (initial advice) or level 2 (casework). You can check whether the person advising you is qualified and to which level. They will refer you to other services if the case is too complex.

Immigration rules

The immigration rules change fairly often, so it can be hard to keep up to date. This information is a general guide to the system currently in place. In the time it takes for this book to be published, further changes may well have come into force. For the latest definitive and reliable information, use the following sources of information.

- www.ukba.homeoffice.gov.uk
- www.ukcisa.org.uk

> 66 For visa applications, it is very important to make sure that you have someone from the school that can help you with your questions and to ask about the appropriate documents needed. Crosscheck the documents with the school to lessen the risk of being rejected. 99
>
> *Nadya Pramudita, Indonesia*

> 66 Having an agent really helped because everything was arranged by them. My only responsibility was to fill in the form and hand it in personally. No interviews or anything. It took around three days to get my approved visa. 99
>
> *Cynthia Cheah, Malaysia*

> 66 Applying for the visa was much more difficult than I imagined it would be. My first application was rejected because I didn't provide my original high school diploma, only a copy of it. Also, leave plenty of time to apply, as my visa got lost in the mail and we had to track down the truck carrying it and meet them in order to get it in on time. 99
>
> *Alexa Johnson, US*

Who needs a visa?

Students coming to the UK from the EEA and Switzerland are entitled to enter the UK freely so will not need entry clearance.

Students classed as visa nationals must apply for a visa, or permission to enter the UK.

Although non-visa nationals do not normally need visas, they are not guaranteed entry into the UK. If you are a non-visa national coming to the UK for more than six months, you will need entry clearance; you should apply from home for an entry certificate. It is recommended that you apply for an entry certificate even if your course is shorter than six months, as this reduces the chance of being turned away at the border. British citizens who live overseas may also need to gain entry clearance before arrival.

To find out which category you fall into, complete the simple questionnaire at www.ukba.homeoffice.gov.uk/visas-immigration/do-you-need-a-visa.

Your permission will normally be valid for the length of the course, with some time before and after (between an additional seven days to four months) depending on how long you are studying here.

Types of student visa

If more than one of the immigration routes applies to you, consider talking to your institution about the pros and cons of each. Young people aged 16 or 17 should discuss whether to apply through Tier 4 (General) or Tier 4 (Child).

If you are already in the UK on another type of visa and decide you wish to study here, speak to the institution where you wish to study. In some cases, you may need to return home to apply for the relevant visa.

Tier 4 (points-based system)

The UK operates a points-based immigration system for all visas and work permits, with Tier 4 relating specifically to students. Different Tier 4 applications are available for adults and children (aged 17 and under).

You need 40 points to gain immigration permission to study in the UK. Ten points are allocated for evidence of sufficient funds and 30 points for a valid Confirmation of Acceptance for Studies (**CAS**) from a UK Border Agency-licensed sponsor. In this case, 'sponsor' refers to your educational institution; it does not refer to financial sponsorship. See p.39 for further details of sponsors and how to find one.

 If our students are refused a visa, it is mainly due to finances.

International officer

The CAS is a reference number from a UK Border Agency database. It is allocated by your institution if they believe you are able to cope academically with the demands of the course (for which they will check your educational background and qualifications) and that you intend to complete your studies (for which they will require the payment of a deposit).

Students need to make a final choice of institution before applying for a student visa. If you haven't made a decision about which institution you will be attending, you could apply as a prospective student while you gather sufficient information to do so.

If you want to change institutions after you receive your visa, things can get complicated, costly and time-consuming. The changes may delay your start date, so it is advisable to research your options thoroughly beforehand.

The points-based system can be somewhat inflexible. If you make a mistake, your form is liable to be rejected. On the positive side, if you complete the application carefully, following the guidelines and providing the correct evidence, then you are likely to be granted a visa.

Financial evidence for Tier 4 visa

In order to receive a Tier 4 visa, you will need to prove that you have money for the course fees, unless you have already paid them. If you will be studying for under a year you will need to show you have the full fees. If the course is over one year, you will need to show you have the fees for the first year. You will also need to show that you can support yourself financially in terms of maintenance or living expenses. You will have to demonstrate that you have £800 per month (or £1,000 per month in inner London) for up to a maximum of nine months. Students who have already studied in the UK and have an established presence may have to provide evidence of maintenance for only two months. The rules regarding established presence can be unclear and should be discussed with your UK institution.

From April 2013, Tier 4 visa application fees for the main applicant are:

- £289 if applying from outside the UK
- £394 if applying by post from within the UK
- £716 if applying in person in the UK.

It is no longer enough to hold the appropriate amount of money for just a short time. You will have to declare that you will continue to hold the maintenance funds to support yourself; this may be checked. Those nationalities classed as low risk will be treated more favourably. Current low-risk nationalities include British nationals overseas, along with people from:

- Argentina
- Australia
- Brunei
- Canada
- Chile
- Croatia
- Hong Kong
- Japan
- New Zealand
- Singapore
- South Korea
- Taiwan
- Trinidad and Tobago
- United States of America.

The UK Border Agency also keeps lists of financial institutions that are unsuitable for providing financial evidence; using a bank that is not approved will mean you won't get the required points for funding. Money can be held in your bank account or the bank account of a parent or legal guardian. Incorrect evidence of finances is a common reason for rejection. Carefully check the guidance notes to the application to ensure that any evidence you provide will be acceptable.

Although you need to provide evidence of fees for the first year only, in practice you will need to find the money to pay for the full length of your course. Similarly, the £800–£1,000 per month that needs to be evidenced may not be enough for you to live on. You need to ensure that you can pay your fees for the full course and support yourself adequately while you are in the UK; if not, you may end up wasting money if you can't remain in the UK to complete your course.

Student visitor visa

If you are planning to visit the UK and wish to undertake a short course, you can do so (with restrictions) if you apply as a student visitor. Young people aged under 18 and wishing to do the same can apply as a child visitor. Your stay on a student visitor visa will be limited to six months (unless you are studying an English-only course) and cannot be extended for full-time or further study. Currently, visitors attending English language courses in the UK can apply for a visa of up to 11 months, but this is for a limited time only and it is not known when this extension will be withdrawn. In all cases, any study undertaken needs to be at an accredited, inspected, reliable institution.

Under the student visitor visa, there is no permission to work in any capacity, whether paid or voluntary. If you intend to take a longer course, you want to work or complete a work placement or you need the flexibility to extend your visa, you should consider the Tier 4 points-based system.

Prospective student visa

A number of the student case studies in this book emphasise the importance of visiting a campus to really discover whether it is right for you. Some universities like potential students to attend an interview. In these cases, a visit to the UK on a prospective student visa might be required. This gives you the opportunity to come to the UK for up to six months in order to complete arrangements for study. If you have already been offered an unconditional place which you intend to accept, then you should apply under Tier 4 of the points-based system.

You should already have made contact with institutions and have an idea of the type and purpose of your studies. You will have to show that studies will commence within six months. Once in the UK, you may then wish to switch to Tier 4, although the fees for applying from within the UK are higher and it can take longer.

When and where to apply

Applications made under Tier 4, by prospective students, or by visa nationals wishing to come as student visitors should be made outside the UK at your local British visa centre. Applications can be made by email, by post or in person, depending on where you live. Non-visa nationals may be able to gain a student visitor visa at the border, while Tier 4 extension applications can be made from within the UK.

You cannot enter the UK until a visa has been issued; since there are no guaranteed timescales for processing, the UK Border Agency advises against making confirmed or non-flexible travel plans until a visa is received. Processing times vary depending on where you are applying from. Take a look at www.ukba. homeoffice.gov.uk/visas-imigration/general-info/processing-times to discover the latest timescales. Bear in mind that processing times are likely to be longer during the summer (June, July and August) in readiness for most courses starting in September.

Applications from outside the UK should be made from three months before the course starts.

What else is needed?

You should start by completing the latest application form, following the guidance notes step by step. Be sure to complete the required appendices and include the following:

- passport or travel document
- the fee in local currency – see www.ukba.homeoffice. gov.uk/aboutus/fees for more details
- biometric details, including fingerprints and a digital photograph, taken at a British visa centre
- a passport-sized photograph, following the guidelines
- all the documents specified in the Tier 4 guidance.
  - This may include certificates and bank statements.
  - All documents should be originals rather than copies.
  - An English translation should be provided, if the original is not in English or Welsh.

The UK Border Agency may make a decision based purely on your application and supporting evidence, so it is essential that you complete your application fully and honestly. Make sure you include all supporting evidence, as without it your application will be rejected. Withheld information, fraudulent information or false documentation will lead to refusal and a possible ban from the UK.

Why might my visa application be declined?

Common reasons for refusal include:

- lack of the correct evidence of funds
- unsuccessful payment of application fees (try to avoid using a credit or debit card)
- failing to include the required supporting documents or approved translations.

ATAS certificate

The **Academic Technology Approval Scheme** (**ATAS**) was introduced to deal with the threat of weapons of mass destruction and to maintain the security of the UK. If you are studying or researching a relevant subject (including specific subjects allied to medicine, sciences, maths, engineering and technology), need a visa and plan to study at postgraduate level (or carry out research for over six months), then you will need an ATAS certificate. The certificate is needed before you can apply for a visa. Check whether your subject is included on the Foreign and Commonwealth Office website at www.fco.gov.uk/en/about-us/what-we-do/services-we-deliver/atas/who-atas.

Changes to the student visa rules

Over the past year, a number of changes have been made to the student visa system. The aim is that students should come to the UK for a limited period and focus on study (rather than work). It is hoped that the new system will eliminate abuse, while still enabling genuine students to study in the UK. Fewer visas will be issued, entry criteria will be tougher, and there will be limits to working and restrictions on working after studying.

The headlines may suggest that this is all bad news, but there are some positive aspects and the changes have not been as severe as anticipated. The changes prioritise quality and genuine education providers; this should reduce the number of bogus colleges, making things safer for students. The educational establishments of the UK still fully recognise that international students bring a great deal to the education system of the UK. Colleges and universities are likely to be competing for fewer students, which should bring benefits to those who are offered a place. If you are a genuine student applying to a reputable institution with the required levels of education and the funds to support yourself, you should still be able to get a visa.

The key changes are as follows.

- Any institution wanting to sponsor students will need to be recognised as a Highly Trusted Sponsor. By the end of 2012, all institutions will need to be accredited by a statutory education inspection body. (Private institutions will be able to work in partnership with licensed sponsors.)
- Students coming to study at degree level now need English at CEFR level B2, rather than the current B1.

- Students intending to study at any institution other than a publicly funded university must have their language assessed by means of a **Secure English Language Test** (**SELT**).
- Students arriving in the UK who cannot speak English and who therefore don't meet the minimum requirements may be refused entry at the border.
- Applicants will have to sign a declaration stating that they have genuine access to appropriate maintenance funding.
- Applicants from low-risk countries will have to provide less financial evidence, although they will still have to declare their access to relevant funds.
- Students at universities and publicly funded colleges will retain the right to work (20 hours per week at universities and 10 hours at public colleges), but students at other institutions will not be able to work.
- A maximum of three years can now be spent studying below degree level (National Qualification Framework levels 3 to 5).
- A maximum of five years can now be spent studying at higher levels (National Qualification Framework levels 6 and 7), with certain exceptions for PhDs and professional qualifications in subjects such as medicine or architecture.
- Only graduates with a skilled job offer from a sponsoring employer can stay on after their course and work in the UK, through the **Tier 2** system; they will need to be in the UK when their student visa expires.
- Only postgraduate students on courses at least 12 months long and government-sponsored students will be able to bring their dependants.

- Prospective student entrepreneurs will have a new
  special visitor category giving them the opportunity to
  remain in the UK to see through new business ideas.

Read the UK Border Agency's *Statement of Intent and
Transitional Measures* for further details of changes and
when they will be introduced. You can find this at www.ukba.
homeoffice.gov.uk/sitecontent/documents/news/sop4.pdf.

Meeting the visa requirements

Once your visa is granted, there are still a number of rules you
must follow so as not to breach the terms of your visa. Initially,
this means arriving on time and registering with your college or
university. You university will need current contact details and
will monitor your attendance and progress. Failure to register
and to attend classes will result in your institution reporting you
to the UK Border Agency; they are obliged to do so.

In order to follow all the correct procedures, remember to:

- inform your institution of any changes, including
  deferring your start date, declining your place or
  changing address
- attend your classes, notifying the institution
  of absences
- work hard at your studies
- obtain permission if you need any time off.

New College Nottingham
www.ncn.ac.uk

New College Nottingham (ncn) is one of the largest Further Education colleges in the UK, with a wide choice of study programmes. The size and diversity of the college ensures an interesting student mix, reflecting a range of cultures, with many international students adding to the vibrant, cosmopolitan atmosphere. Nottingham is an excellent place to study. *The Virgin Guide to British Universities* (2010) states: "Nottingham is without doubt the best city in the country for a student". Nottingham is located in heart of the UK with all other major cities within easy reach and is well known around the world for the legend of Robin Hood.

ncn offers a range of programmes including university-level courses, A-Levels, further education, international foundation programmes, and English language tuition.

International students at ncn receive excellent support from an experienced and dedicated International support team, which is able to help with all aspects of life in the UK, including accommodation, visa advice, and much more.

There are many benefits to studying at New College Nottingham. Our courses open up a wide variety of opportunities for future career development, progression to further or higher education, as well as improving English language skills.

New College Nottingham has a long history of teaching English to students from around the world through its dedicated English language academy, the Nottingham English School (www.nottinghmenglishschool. com). English provision is validated by the British Council and includes English courses throughout the year, pre-sessional English, a Summer School programme, and tailor-made programmes to suit individual groups.

Contact us to find out more or visit the website:

New College Nottingham
Telephone: +44 (0) 115 9104610 / 9104615 / 9104668
Email: international@ncn.ac.uk
www.ncn.ac.uk

Nottingham English School
Telephone: +44 (0) 115 9104615
Email: nes@ncn.ac.uk
www.nottinghamenglishschool.com

Case Study

Sofiia Bondarchuk

Sofiia came from the Ukraine to study an International Business Foundation course at ncn before moving onto a Foundation Degree in Law. With family living in the Nottingham area and the College offering flexible study options, New College Nottingham was the perfect fit.

"I really enjoy my studies. The tutors are brilliant. They make lessons enjoyable, but I'm learning at the same time. The International team have been great too. They helped me settle in and offered me language support when I first arrived. Now they help me with essays and advise me which books to buy – it's like they are a part of my family!

"Outside the classroom there are many things to get involved with at ncn. I took up pottery and rock climbing and the activities have been really good for meeting people in a relaxed setting. Now I have a great social life, with friends from all over the world.

"Nottingham is a great city – it's just the right size. There is shopping, entertainment, churches and museums all in walking distance of each other. The people are really helpful too and always smiling. It's got everything you need!"

Chapter 9
Accommodation

Accommodation is one of the major concerns for students from overseas. It is important to have somewhere safe and comfortable to live and it can really make a difference when adjusting to life in the UK. Although it can be difficult to be sure that you are making the right housing choices from a distance, you should try to arrange some accommodation, even if it is on a temporary basis, before you get to the UK.

Help from your institution

Your college or university is likely to be involved in the process of arranging accommodation and will send you information on the range of options on offer. As there is a shortage of affordable student housing in much of the UK, it is advisable to discuss the matter with the university as soon as possible. Some institutions guarantee accommodation for the first or subsequent years of study, provided you apply by certain key dates; make sure you don't miss these deadline dates. It may be that you have special requirements, perhaps because of a disability or because you are bringing your family with you to the UK. If so, it is even more important to have early discussions about where you will live.

Every year, international students are conned out of money after responding to fraudulent requests to send money from overseas. It is unsafe to send money for private accommodation from overseas; you should never pay money for private accommodation unless you have seen it first.

To avoid fraud, try to arrange accommodation through your college or university. If you are too late to find university accommodation, get advice from your college or university about reputable accommodation providers or discuss alternative short-term solutions.

Costs

Your accommodation costs are likely to be your largest monthly expense, so think about how much you can afford to spend and what your budget will be. When comparing options, remember to find out what is included and think about what you will need to provide. For example, staying in catered accommodation will mean you won't have to pay for food or buy cooking equipment. Ask whether your bills will be included or whether this is an additional expense you will need to budget for. You will need to consider whether you need accommodation for 52 weeks of the year.

The options

There is a range of different options on offer to students. Which option works best for you will depend on you as a person and your needs as a student. You may want to start off by asking your chosen institution what it has available. A small college or university may have more limited choices than one of the larger institutions.

Halls of residence

Halls of residence are accommodation blocks offering private study bedrooms to large numbers of students. Rooms will be grouped together around some shared facilities. Some halls offer the option to share a room, which can reduce costs. Many halls are owned by the university, although private halls also exist, offering similar facilities at broadly similar costs. Most halls will be aimed at students from one particular university, although a few institutions offer halls to students from a range of individual universities. Halls of residence are worth considering, particularly as international students are often given priority in this type of accommodation, and halls offer a chance to meet fellow students in a safe setting.

Standards and prices range widely, although they should all meet minimum standards, regardless of who runs them.

Facilities

A single room should contain a single bed and mattress, a wardrobe, desk, desk chair and storage space. Some rooms have their own washbasin. Students will need to supply their own bedding, although you may be able to purchase this through your university. Some halls offer facilities for couples or families, but there may be limited places available.

Bathroom and kitchens tend to be shared, although some halls are en suite, where students have their own bathroom facilities (shower, washbasin and toilet). Newer accommodation can sometimes resemble a basic hotel, offering en suite, telephone and internet access. You are likely to have a basic cleaning service and you may find laundry facilities on site. There should be access to a shared public telephone.

Some halls of residence are for both men and women (mixed), with other halls just for males or just for females (single sex). When you apply for accommodation you will be able to state your preference.

Catered or self-catered

In self-catered accommodation, you share kitchen facilities with a group of fellow students. Large appliances will be provided (cooker, fridge, freezer and sometimes a kettle, microwave and toaster) but you will need to bring cutlery, plates, bowls, cups, pots and pans, tea towels and so on. You will also need to buy your own food, so consider how close you are to the nearest supermarkets and shops. Sharing facilities requires some tolerance and understanding.

Students pay extra for catered halls of residence. This tends to include breakfast and evening meals every day with lunch included at weekends. Meals will be offered at set times of the day, which can be restrictive, and the food can be basic and uninspiring. On the plus side, you will not need to spend time on shopping and cooking or spend money on food and kitchen equipment. Some universities offer catered halls with the facility to take your meals at a variety of settings on the university campus, providing a much more flexible option. Others have a semi-catered option where you get an evening meal included, but make your own arrangement for breakfast and lunch. Students who are catered for should still get access to some kitchen facilities for making drinks or small snacks.

Costs

The price you pay per week varies and is often a reflection of the number of facilities available and the convenience of the location. Prices for the cheapest self-catered halls range from about £55 per week upwards; many start somewhere around £70 to £90, although you could easily end up paying over £100 per week.

The cheapest catered halls will cost from about £100 per week, although £200 is not uncommon. Accommodation in London is the most expensive. Don't forget to factor in additional travel costs if you are far from your place of study.

Length of residency

Some halls offer a range of options for residency. Many international students favour a year-round residency. As an alternative, you may be able to stay during term time and in the Christmas and Easter holidays, but leave for the summer holidays. Some home students will choose the option of term time only – normally 31 weeks per year – meaning that facilities can be more limited outside term time. It is important to plan ahead when choosing your options. When you sign your contract at the beginning of the academic year, you need to be sure that the accommodation is going to suit your needs. Paying for 51 weeks' accommodation if you are only going to use it for 31 weeks is a huge waste of money. You are likely to need to pay for halls of residence on a termly basis, normally three times per year.

Pros and cons

There can be downsides to living with large numbers of people, most notably noise, disruption and milk disappearing from the communal fridge. Halls of residence will have staff to deal with issues and any problems. The rooms tend to be functional and institutional in style, although you can personalise them with your own things.

On the upside, halls can be a very sociable experience, with parties and social events. You will have the chance to meet lots of fellow students, some of whom may be on your course, and you can start to build a network of support around you.

Some of the benefits of halls of residence include:

- an easy way to meet friends and fellow students
- bills are included, making budgeting easier
- the option for catered or self-catered accommodation
- social events
- a chance to meet friends from many different cultures and backgrounds.

Some postgraduate students choose to apply for the position of hall tutor or senior resident within the halls of residence for a small salary or discounted accommodation. The role might involve being on call on a rota basis overnight or arranging sporting and social events, as well as taking responsibility for the well-being of a number of tutees.

Homestay

The chance to stay with a host family is often offered to those under 18 or those coming to the UK for a shorter period, but it can also be a great option for any student coming for longer periods of time. Unlike some of the other choices, **homestay** will immerse you in British life and culture. You can practise your English every day as you converse with your hosts.

Host families

There is no such thing as a typical British family. Host families come from a diverse range of backgrounds: retired, working, with or without children and pets, single parents and so on. What host families have in common is the ability to speak English and the desire to welcome students into their home. Accommodation offices will do their best to match you to hosts who suit your needs and preferences.

Host families are checked to ensure that what they provide is clean, hygienic and suitable. They are assessed to make sure that they meet required standards; assessment may be carried out by the university or college or through a private agency.

Costs and facilities

Students will be expected to sign an agreement relating to the payment of rent and a deposit, as well as the period of notice required if you decide to leave. The deposit is there to cover any damage, loss of keys or rent arrears.

Homestay tends to be more expensive than renting, with the cheapest prices ranging from about £100 per week (catered), but this option is likely to provide you with more benefits. You can expect your own private room including a bed, bedding and storage. You should get space to study, although wireless internet isn't available everywhere. Lighting and heating will be provided for you and will be included in your accommodation costs. You will get access to shared toilet and washing facilities that you can use in private. Living areas, such as lounges or dining rooms, are likely to be communal areas shared with the family.

Many homestays are offered on a half-board basis including breakfast and an evening meal every day plus lunch at the weekends. You should have access to a telephone to receive calls at reasonable times and will normally have internet access. There may be additional charges to use these facilities, and usage will be agreed between the hosts and the student.

> **❝** Don't be shy: come out and have a conversation and get to know the family. Don't hesitate to ask if you don't understand anything. **❞**
>
> *Minami Eto, Japan*

Pros and cons

This option is not for everyone. You are likely to be eating with the family and sharing communal areas of their home, so it is important that you are able to get along. Patience and respect are needed on both sides as you get used to living together. You need to be mature enough to communicate effectively and discuss any needs that you may have. You may need to be flexible on some issues. The food and the culture may be different from your previous experiences, so some time to adjust may be needed. If you do have problems that you can't resolve, your international office or accommodation office contacts are there to help.

If you are looking for accommodation right on the doorstep of your university, then homestay may not fulfil your needs. Institutions may have host families living in a range of areas, so you could have to travel to your place of study. You can ask about distance from the institution when you discuss the matter with your international office or accommodation office.

> **"** I ask my students to make a list of foods they don't eat (and those they don't like) to pass on to their host family. **"**
>
> *International officer*

Consider what type of person you are. If you crave total independence, then this option may not suit you. You will have to follow the rules of the household and consider the needs of the host family. But if you like the idea of learning more about real life in your host country and would prefer the comfort of a "home from home", then homestay is hard to beat.

The uncertainty of staying with someone you don't know may discourage you from this option, but many students recommend homestay. Positive homestay experiences can be a real source of personal support a long way from home.

Some of the benefits of homestay include:

- the chance to improve your English more quickly
- the opportunity to gain a greater understanding of the British way of life
- meals and bills are likely to be included, making budgeting easier
- access to the local knowledge of your hosts
- a supported way to start your student life in the UK
- the chance to make lifelong friends.

Hostels

Hostels are often popular as a short-term option for international students. Most hostels for medium to long stays tend to be limited to London. Your university or college will have information about any hostels near your institution.

In the capital, there are a wide range and variety of hostels; some are commercial while others are run by charitable organisations; some are for men or women only, while others accept families. Most hostels offer some type of dormitory accommodation where rooms are shared; many offer more private facilities too. As with halls, some offer en suite facilities with toilet, shower and washbasin leading off your room, but you will pay a premium for the convenience. Some hostels are aimed specifically at particular nationalities or religions, while others are more open.

As hostels are not university-owned, you will get the chance to live with a wider range of people; they can be great places to meet a variety of students from other universities and colleges. It is important to note that most hostels aren't aimed just at students, though, so you should check the details carefully. If you have a long list of requirements you may have more limited choice, so it is advisable to start looking early.

Some of the benefits of hostels include:

- often a short-term option
- the most choice can be found in London
- you can find facilities to meet your needs
- a good way to get to know your local area before finding more long-term accommodation.

> If you need a short-term solution, hostels, homestays or bed and breakfasts might keep you going until you find something more permanent.

Bedsits

If the previous options don't seem to offer the privacy that you need, then you could consider a **bedsit** (or, to give it its full title, a bed-sitting room). A bedsit is a single room with sleeping, living and often cooking facilities in the one space. The furnishings and facilities can be fairly basic. Occupants often share a bathroom (and sometimes a kitchen). You are responsible for your own cooking, cleaning and laundry. Remember to find out about the length of your contract, whether you pay monthly or termly, and whether any bills will be included. You should always take a look around a bedsit before renting, as standards can vary.

Bedsits can be an affordable way to rent your own accommodation, but the benefits in privacy may be outweighed by the lack of company. Unlike in halls, you will not have access to a communal or social area. Unlike in student hostels, you won't necessarily have other like-minded students living next door. Bedsits are often converted from residential housing. You may have no links with the other occupants there, so it is not guaranteed to be the most sociable of places.

Some of the benefits of bedsits include:

- an affordable way to rent private accommodation
- privacy
- independence.

Renting flats and houses

Once you have made friends and you are happy to live together, a rented flat or house can be the next step. Students usually rent out furnished properties with furniture and large kitchen appliances provided. These may be owned by the university or by a private landlord, ranging from an individual with one house to let to a large company with hundreds of properties.

Facilities

Most shared accommodation like this is made up of a shared kitchen, bathroom and living space, with a bedroom each. Unlike hostels and halls, you have some say over who you choose to share your communal spaces with.

Costs

Renting a shared flat or house requires the most responsibility, budgeting and planning skills of all the accommodation options. You may be working together to shop, cook and clean, and sharing the bills between you. You are likely to have to pay your own electricity, gas, telephone, TV licence and internet costs. It is sensible to discuss in advance how you will divide the bills. What happens if someone uses the phone all the time for expensive calls home? Or if someone doesn't contribute to payments for food shopping? How will you solve these problems? It is often better to discuss these potential issues in advance.

If everyone in residence is a student, you will not need to pay Council Tax (a tax paid to your local government authority to pay for rubbish collection, street lighting, police and fire services, schools and so on). UKCISA has a useful information sheet on Council Tax at www.ukcisa.org.uk.

In Northern Ireland, people pay rates rather than Council Tax; your tenancy agreement should explain who is liable to pay the rates and whether the cost is included in the rent. Find out more from your university or Housing Advice Northern Ireland at www.housingadviceni.org/rates.

Most private, rented accommodation will be paid for in advance on a monthly basis, although some landlords who work mainly with students may ask for termly payments. The landlord may be looking for students to sign a contract for an academic year, from September onwards. You may be expected to pay some money over the summer to reserve a house from September. Check all these details, as you need to be sure that the contract meets your needs as an international student.

Renting safely

Your accommodation office can tell you more about the standards that accommodation needs to meet and may provide a checklist for you to work through. Some universities work with landlords and local authorities to check that properties are accredited, that necessary safety checks have been carried out and that the following are available:

- a valid gas safety certificate
- a valid electrical safety certificate
- a fire extinguisher and fire blanket

- a smoke alarm
- a carbon monoxide detector.

Some landlords can be unscrupulous and may not always repair things promptly or provide you with adequate furniture or appliances. Whenever possible, it is best to use a landlord that your college or institution approves. It may mean that you have some additional protection if things go wrong. On the whole, most landlords are good and should treat you fairly, but extra care should be taken to protect yourself when renting privately.

There are certain things that you will need to check to determine whether you are happy to sign the contract and move in.

- Look around the property, checking that it is in a reasonable condition and is secure.
- Find out whether the property is located in a safe neighbourhood.
- Check the details of your tenancy agreement.
  - How much is the rent?
  - What does it include?
  - How much is the deposit?
  - How long does the agreement last?
  - How soon can you move in?
- Check the **inventory**, making a note of missing or damaged items and informing the landlord.
- Check who will be responsible for repairs.
- Find out who is responsible for bills and how much they are likely to be.
- Get a receipt or rent book for any money that you pay.

Tenancies

Many private rentals will be under some form of shorthold tenancy or assured tenancy, depending on where you live. These tenancies do not relate to university-owned halls of residence, but will apply to private rentals like bedsits, private halls and shared flats or houses. Different rules apply if your landlord lives in the building. The housing charity, Shelter, has useful information on this subject:

- England: http://england.shelter.org.uk
- Scotland: http://scotland.shelter.org.uk
- Wales: www.sheltercymru.org.uk
- Northern Ireland: www.housingadviceni.org.

> There are variations in housing law across the countries of the UK. Make sure you check what applies to your accommodation.

Some of the benefits of renting shared flats and houses include:

- a combination of privacy and company
- an affordable way to rent private accommodation
- independence.

Paying a deposit

In addition to paying at least one month's rent in advance, most accommodation will require a deposit, often equivalent to a month's rent, to be held until your tenancy is over. The money will then be returned to you provided there has been no damage. Normal wear and tear should not lead to the loss of your deposit.

At the beginning of your contract, you should check carefully through the inventory (the list of the property and its contents). Make sure you agree to what you are signing. You and the landlord can take photographs of the accommodation as evidence of the condition when you arrive. Look out for damage or items in poor condition, as these may lead to disputes if not clearly documented.

When you come to leave, make sure all rent and bills are paid. Make sure you haven't caused any damage. Leave the property in a clean and tidy condition.

> Remember that you will normally need to hand over the equivalent of two months' rent (one month's rent in advance and the equivalent to one month's rent as a deposit) to secure a contract or tenancy agreement.

Some landlords have been known to retain or delay the return of a tenant's deposit. If you rent through an assured or shorthold tenancy, you will be eligible for your deposit to be protected. In England, Wales and Scotland, a tenancy deposit protection scheme is in operation to make sure that any deposit paid to a private landlord is kept safe. (No such scheme is in place in Northern Ireland as yet, although one is expected before the end of 2012.) If there is a dispute over the deposit, it can normally be resolved through this scheme. Some schemes result in a slight delay to the deposits being returned. If you are returning to your home country, it may be possible to get your deposit returned overseas for a small charge.

International students with families

It can be a challenge to find affordable accommodation for families, so plan ahead. You should make sure you have some accommodation booked for your family before you arrive. One way to do this is to initially visit alone in order to view properties and secure somewhere to live. Depending on your circumstances, this may require a visa. See Chapter 8 on visas for details (p.125).

Some institutions have space for couples and families in their own halls or university-owned accommodation, while others might be limited to referring you to hostels in the interim and private accommodation thereafter. Remember that you need to view private accommodation before paying anything, so you cannot secure this from overseas. Use the international or accommodation services of the university or college to help you with this process.

Choosing your accommodation

When deciding on the most appropriate type of accommodation, you should ask yourself the following questions.

- How much money do I have to spend?
- What facilities do I need?
- How close to the institution do I want to be?
- How much privacy do I like?
- How much independence do I need?
- Do I want to cook for myself?
- What happens during the holidays?
- What is included within the price?
- What else will I need to budget for?

Use the expertise of your institution for support and guidance with the process, making sure that you use providers of accommodation who have been approved, accredited or recommended by your institution whenever possible.

Insurance

Regardless of your type of accommodation, you will need to protect yourself against loss of or damage to your belongings. A range of different providers offer insurance policies. UKCISA and the National Union of Students both recommend Endsleigh Insurance (www.endsleigh.co.uk/student).

STUDENT STORY
Minami Eto, Japan

Minami Eto is 17 and from Chiba in Japan. She is still in high school and has spent the past 10 months studying at a further education college in the UK as part of an exchange programme. "Coming to England has been my dream ever since I was a child. Learning English was necessary for me, as I hope to work as cabin crew when I finish high school."

Minami's school has links with Sheffield College. "The international officer came to Japan to explain the programme. I had information from the college so I knew what to expect." The international officer has been one of Minami's main sources of support during her stay in England.

Minami didn't find the process of applying for a visa too difficult, receiving help with the procedures from her school. "I had to get a student visa, but fortunately I got one right away."

In order to gain her place at the college, Minami had to complete a college application form and take some tests in English fluancy while in Japan. She and two fellow students from her high school were successful in gaining places.

When she arrived in Sheffield, Minami found that her level of English had already started to improve. "When I came here, I had to do the same English tests again to decide which course level was right for me. The teacher told me I did better when I got here!

"When I first came I was very nervous, but my host family and the college helped me." Getting used to the local accent took some adjustment too. "I couldn't understand and people spoke too fast."

She received plenty of support from a range of people. "My teacher took me on a tour of the city centre, showing me the shops, the station and so on. That was really helpful." Minami feels very lucky to have been placed with such a supportive host family. "I was really worried, not knowing them and what they would be like, but they were very nice." She advises against staying in your room the whole time. "Don't be shy: come out and have a conversation and get to know the family. Don't hesitate to ask if you don't understand."

Minami has been getting used to English food. "English and Japanese foods are quite different. I didn't expect English food to be nice. My family and friends told me it might not be good, but it is not as bad as I expected. I really like fishcakes. To start with, I found English food was too sweet, but I am used to it now. My friends and family send me packages with food from Japan."

The financial side of life in the UK hasn't been too difficult, as the costs for most things are comparable. Minami recommends using a student card to get discounts on transport, clothes and the cinema.

One big difference that Minami noticed was how quiet the city centre can be in the evenings compared with Japan. "I was surprised. At home it is really busy and crowded, so I felt a little bit scared." As Minami is under 18, there are various rules that she has to follow. "I can't go to visit another country as I'm under 18. I have visited many cities, but I have to get the permission of the college, my high school and my parents before visiting another city. I also have to be home at 10 o'clock. Back home I wouldn't have to be home at 10 o'clock."

On the whole, she feels she has adjusted well. "It hasn't been too difficult. The food was a difficult part. Speaking and communicating were difficult and still can be difficult. I was surprised to see people from so many different cultures. When I sit on the bus I can see people from all over the world. It's different in Japan."

She feels she has benefited from the different style of teaching. "In a classroom in Japan, the teacher talks and the students listen. Here we always discuss and give our own opinions. I can learn well and improve through saying what I'm thinking and giving my opinions."

Minami used many websites to help her find out about visiting the UK. You could start with the website for VisitBritain, the national tourism agency, at www.visitbritain.com.

Minami has lots of positive things to say about the whole experience. "It's good to go to another country, to learn many things, not only the language but culture from all over the world. I have learned how different things are from in my own country."

And the best bits about her time here? "I have learned many things I couldn't learn in Japan. I have met people from all over the world. For a teenager, it's good to know these things at a young age; to learn all these things and improve myself at such a young age is especially good."

Minami will soon return to Japan to continue high school, so is she looking forward to going home? "Half and half!"

Uxbridge College

Uxbridge is a great place for an international student to live and work, and Uxbridge College welcomes students from around the world.

We are only 20 kilometres from London with direct underground train links to the city centre, and very close to Heathrow, the UK's biggest international airport. The area around Uxbridge is multiculturally diverse and most nationalities find a 'home from home' community in London while they are here.

Uxbridge College is one of the top government-funded colleges in London, with Highly Trusted status on the UK Border Agency's Register of Sponsors, which is licensed under Tier 4 of the UK Border Agency's points-based system. The college is regularly inspected by UK government quality agencies including Ofsted, QAA and the British Council, and Ofsted gave the college an outstanding rating, the highest possible grade.

Why choose Uxbridge College?

- **A safe and welcoming college** – we take every step to ensure your safety, health and well-being. We welcome students whatever their background and previous experience.
- **Top-class staff** – our teaching staff are highly qualified, many with significant industry experience. You can learn the skills employers demand from industry experts.
- **Fantastic facilities** – we have invested £11 million in the last year in developing the college to ensure that you go to study in top quality classrooms, studios and workshops. We recently opened our new £6 million sports and leisure facilities and a £5 million IT and media block. We have also developed the social spaces on both campuses providing new and improved areas for students to relax in.

- **Curriculum support** – Uxbridge College provides a range of pre-university programmes and Pathway to Degree courses that can help students gain entry to university. Our Pathway to Degree programmes are designed to fast-track students onto the second or third year of an undergraduate degree. There is a range of subjects to choose from and these programmes offer a flexible and affordable way to study a university-level course. Fees for higher education courses at Uxbridge College are far lower than those charged by many universities, for the same level of study and high-quality qualifications.

We offer a free 'meet and greet' service for new international students where you are picked up from any London airport and taken to where you will be staying within Greater London and the surrounding area.

For more information please contact the International Office on:
+44(0)1895 853 469
international@uxbridgecollege.ac.uk.

Case study

Smit Parmar, India, Engineering student

Progressed to: University of Greenwich, BEng (Hons) in Electrical and Electronic Engineering

"I am from India, and completed my Electrical Engineering Diploma over there. Engineering is my passion, and I found that the HND in Electrical & Electronic Engineering at Uxbridge College was the most appropriate course for me.

"All my tutors were very helpful in each and every aspect of my course – we did not have to book an appointment to meet them, and we could go and see them with any problems we were facing. They had vast experience in the engineering industry, and knew about the opportunities once you had completed your studies – as a student it was important for me to know what I could be doing once I finished the course.

"Choosing the HND also meant that I could jump directly to the final year on a university degree course, and by doing that I saved time and money. I developed so many skills during my time at Uxbridge College, and in my opinion it is worth choosing Uxbridge College because it gives you a chance to identify the right career and provides you with the opportunities to achieve your desired goals."

Chapter 10
Travelling to and arriving in the UK

As the start date of your course approaches, it is time to consider your preparations for travelling to and arriving in the UK. This chapter includes tips on preparing to travel and on helping you adjust to a new culture and way of life, as well as looking at how you can prepare yourself for the challenges of UK study.

Before you travel

You will have a long list of things to do before you set off for the UK. If you need a visa or entry clearance, remember to apply for this in advance. Make sure you also have a valid passport. Collect original copies of certificates and exam results from your school and university; arrange for their official translation into English if necessary. Bring both originals and official translations with you to the UK; it is prudent to take copies and keep them in a safe place.

Visit your doctor or dentist before you leave your home country. If you have any health conditions or require prescribed medicines, bring a doctor's report translated into English. The report should include details of the condition and the necessary treatment and medication. All students should check with the British embassy or high commission in their home country to determine whether any vaccinations will be required before coming to the UK.

Book travel tickets and take out insurance for travel. Consider how you will transport what you need to the UK. Airlines have varying baggage restrictions and you have to pay for extra baggage; however, it may work out cheaper to pay in advance for an extra suitcase on your flight, rather than posting a large parcel. Take careful note of the restrictions on items that can be brought into the UK. Remember that you can buy most things you will need after you arrive.

It is advisable to bring enough money in British currency (GBP) or traveller's cheques to get you started until you can set up a bank account. An amount of between £200 and £300 is often suggested. Don't carry large amounts of cash, as you won't be able to claim it back if it is stolen. There are currency restrictions in place in certain countries that may limit the amount of money you can take in or out. It might be useful to have a credit card, as long as you can use it in the UK. You will need to talk to your bank about the rules and the costs for transferring money to the UK; make sure you can make international transfers from your bank at home and bring account and contact details for the bank with you.

> **❝** Please don't bring large amounts of cash to the UK to pay your tuition fees. You can pay using a range of methods, but carrying lots of cash is risky. **❞**
>
> *International officer*

Make sure you have read all the information from your university carefully so you are prepared for arrival on the specified date. Depending on what your entry clearance or visa allows, it is useful to arrive around a week before your classes start, in time for any orientation events; your college or university will give you further details. Check that all necessary forms have been completed and returned.

Travelling to the UK checklist

- Passport, including visa or entry clearance (if applicable)
- Tickets
- Money, traveller's cheques and/or a credit card.
- Documents (confirmed offer of a place, evidence of finances for fees and living costs, accommodation paperwork)
- Insurance
- Plans for how to get to your final destination

It is a good idea to make copies of your passport, visa and other important documents, keeping them somewhere safe and separate from the originals.

When you arrive

When you arrive in the UK, you will need to show your passport and visa stamp (or vignette). Make sure you have the documents you used when you applied for your visa in your hand luggage; copies are acceptable. This should include your **CAS** reference number and any other supporting documents.

Immigration officials from the UK Border Agency will talk to you on arrival in the UK, verifying your identity, asking you about the purpose of your visit and checking documentation. You will need to be able to explain the purpose of your visit and hold a simple conversation in English, regardless of whether you have already completed a Secure English Language Test (SELT). If you are unable to do so, they have the right to decline you the right to enter or remain in the UK.

At the busiest times of the year, some institutions will send staff to meet you at the airport, making the final part of your journey stress-free.

Adjusting to the UK

It can be a worrying, and often stressful, time as you adapt to a new country and a different education system. It is natural to feel some anxiety over this process, but you should be reassured that you will receive lots of help from your institution. They will help you when you arrive and even before you get here. On some university websites, you will have the chance to hear international students talking about their experiences. Others use Facebook and offer forums and message boards where you can ask questions and interact with students and staff. Some institutions will offer a system of mentoring or buddying, whereby new students are linked up to those with more experience of the UK. When you get here, there will be social events and chances to meet other international students. Students tend to help one another and form support networks.

> **"** There were current students welcoming new students at the airport, and there were lots of events during freshers' week helping new students get to know the campus and the city. I also got to meet with my adviser of studies, who was there to help with any academic questions and problems. **"**
>
> *David Stoll, Luxembourg*

> **"** The UK is no stranger to international students, and I find that their institutions (not just mine) are well equipped to deal with any issue an international student might have. There are entire offices and support groups set up to help us, and I am extremely grateful for them! The availability of these services lowered my stress levels a great deal in my first couple of weeks here. **"**
>
> *Kimberly Stevenson, US*

Arriving in a new country can be quite a culture shock. No matter how much research you do beforehand, not everything will be quite as you anticipated. In addition to missing home, family and friends, you may have the challenges of a language barrier to contend with. Remember that it is normal to feel this way. Try to give the adjustment process time; come with an open mind and be prepared to be flexible as you get used to a new country and culture.

You can do small things to ease the transition, such as keeping in touch with family and friends, keeping informed of events back home, and making friends with international students from a range of different cultures, who will probably be feeling the same way. Meeting people from the UK will help you gain an understanding of the culture here. Try to make your room feel homely by including personal items, like photographs and mementoes. Getting involved in familiar activities can help, such as sports, cultural interests or faith activities.

> 66 Culture shock is inevitable, but you can lessen the shock. Be aware that some things may be different from the things back home. You may need a couple of months to adapt until you feel completely comfortable with it. 99
>
> *Nadya Pramudita, Indonesia*
>
> 66 I was homesick when I first arrived and I still get homesick. I find it helps to keep busy. I have met good friends who help me when I am feeling sad, some from the UK, some from Europe and the rest of the world. 99
>
> *Andrzej Polewiak, Poland*

Looking after yourself and staying healthy are also important to a successful transition, as illness and exhaustion can exacerbate any problems. Try to get enough sleep, eat a balanced diet and take some exercise. Sometimes some familiar food from home will help. The orientation process arranged by your institution is designed to support you through this tough time. If you find the process harder than anticipated, help is available through international and academic staff, as well as counselling and health services both through your institution and the NHS. Asking for help is not an admission of failure in the UK. These services are here to support you.

Preparing for UK study

Adjusting to a new education system won't happen automatically. It is best to prepare yourself for the changes. If you have been offered an unconditional place on your chosen course, then you already meet the academic entry requirements and level of English required. You may be coming to take a preparatory course to prepare your level of English or your study and research skills. To improve your chances of success at any level, it is good to know as much as you can about the programme you will be studying. You should thoroughly read and understand all the course information and start to work through some of the recommended reading. No matter which country you were educated in, you will find differences in the UK education system. The chapter on the UK system deals with some of the variations (see p.1).

The Prepare for Success website (www.prepareforsuccess.org. uk) covers what to expect from the UK education system in great detail. It is an essential tool to help you know what to expect from study in the UK, providing exercises and activities to help you acclimatise. UKCISA also provides a helpful information sheet on the same subject.

You will need to be prepared for independent study; the higher the level you will be studying at, the greater the challenge. You should be far more of an independent learner by the time you reach doctoral level. You will need strong time management and organisation skills and the ability to retain focus on your studies. If these skills need strengthening, you can talk to your university or college about tips and who can help. It can be useful to talk to others who have recently studied at your level and share ideas with them.

University of Kent

The University of Kent, the UK's European University, is one of the UK's most dynamic universities. It has campuses and centres in Canterbury, Medway, Paris, Brussels and Athens and is a major educational, economic and cultural force throughout the region.

In the UK government's Research Assessment Exercise (RAE), each of Kent's 18 academic schools were judged to produce world-leading and internationally recognised research. This research informs teaching on all courses at Kent, ensuring that every student benefits from advanced and groundbreaking learning.

The international outlook of the institution adds to the cosmopolitan nature of the Kent experience. Excellence in teaching, variety in extracurricular activities, and course-related internship/work experience are well established.

Time spent studying at overseas partner institutions is greatly supported. These opportunities contribute to Kent's excellent graduate employability record, making Kent's graduates among the highest earners for graduate starting salaries.

The Kent experience is unique in higher education, and students consistently vote Kent one of the top universities in the UK in National Student Satisfaction Surveys. At the centre of this experience is the dedication of teachers at Kent. For three years running, National Teaching Fellowships have been awarded to Kent academics in recognition of their outstanding work.

The University of Kent has centres of specialist education in both Brussels (international relations and law) and Paris (art, literature, film and culture). It awards a number of joint degrees and enjoys over 100 partnerships with international institutions.

Kent is ranked among the top 15% of UK universities by both the *Guardian* university league tables and by the Government's Research Assessment Exercise. According to recent *Sunday Times* university guides, University of Kent "can claim to be Britain's only international university" and is "in the top 20 for high-starting salaries".

Case study

Laura Floyd, Belgium/US, Business Administration and Spanish

"The University of Kent certainly has a lot to offer – great academics, countless clubs and teams, a beautiful city and the opportunity to graduate in one of the most iconic cathedrals in the world.

"What attracted me further was the fact that Kent is known as the UK's 'European university'. Coming from an international school background, this particularly caught my eye, as it promised a diverse student body and a way to find a comfort zone with Americans or Belgians when I was feeling homesick.

"It is very easy to find students from your home country for familiarity and to find friends from around the world to make the university experience enjoyable and culturally diverse. The best example I have to illustrate this is through our volleyball club. Volleyball is not a typically British sport, which means that as a club, we mainly attracted international students.

"There are societies that fit almost any interest and nationality. I was lucky enough to attend a rendition of Haydn's Creation by our students in the Canterbury Cathedral!

"Another reason I chose this particular university is that they gave me the option to do a joint degree in Business Administration with Spanish, and because of this course I am spending next year in Spain as part of the Erasmus exchange program.

"Kent has many partner universities all around Europe and in other parts of the world, with whom you can exchange depending on the course you chose. I was looking forward to my course because business and Spanish were two subjects I was interested in, and this only increased through my academic experience here.

"The teaching staff are passionate and approachable."

Chapter 11
Living costs

Financial issues are one of the main concerns for international students. It is expensive to live in the UK, and many students who have studied in the UK report that they underestimated the cost of living here. The UK Border Agency requires students to have £1,000 per month for living costs if they are spending most of their time in inner London, with £800 per month for living costs elsewhere in the UK. Bear in mind that the first few weeks are likely to be the most expensive, as you establish yourself in the UK and buy the things you need to get started with your accommodation and your studies. Remember that you will spend more money on living costs if you live here all year round.

Getting used to UK costs

Examples of prices:

- pint of milk: 50p
- chocolate bar: 60p
- soft drinks can: 70p
- lunch in a café: from £5 for a sandwich, crisps and a drink
- cinema ticket: from £7 at peak times
- local travel:
  - weekly bus ticket: £12
  - taxi: £2.40 for the minimum fare
  - London Underground seven-day student travelcard for zones 1 and 2: £20.40.

Be aware that these prices will vary across the country.

The UNIAID student calculator (www.studentcalculator.org.uk/international) is a great tool for helping you calculate how much money you will need and your likely living costs, so you are advised to use this before you come to the UK.

> **❝❝** Even when you think you've fully adjusted to the GBP system, you're probably still underestimating the value, so keep converting in your head whenever you buy. **❞❞**
>
> *Ami Jones, Hong Kong*

Anticipating costs

Your costs will vary depending on where you live and the type of lifestyle you lead. You may find that your actual costs will be more than the amount required to gain a visa. You need to know beforehand how much money you will need to get by, as there are limits to what you can do if you find yourself in financial hardship. Your institution will be able to tell you more specific costs for accommodation, travel and living costs in your local area. If you know what your expenses are likely to be, you can choose where to spend and where to save your money. Many students do not have much money to spend but can still find ways to manage and enjoy themselves on a budget.

Accommodation

Accommodation costs vary greatly in different regions of the UK and depend on where in the region you choose to live; city-centre living tends to be more expensive, but it may reduce travel costs if you are close to your institution and amenities. London has the highest accommodation costs in the UK.

Excerpt from the NUS/Unipol Accommodation Costs Survey 2009–10

Average weekly rent by city	2008–09	2009–10
Northern Ireland	£59.28	£64.17
Wales	£78.60	£79.40
North West (England)	£79.98	£85.93
East of England	£85.63	£88.79
North East (England)	£86.48	£90.39
West Midlands (England)	£82.05	£93.09
Scotland	£96.35	£102.74
South East (England)	£95.96	£102.90
South West (England)	£96.09	£103.04
East Midlands (England)	£108.69	£112.69
London (England)	£115.56	£125.34

Insurance

You are likely to need various forms of insurance while in the
UK. You may be able to take out insurance from your home
country, although there are many insurance providers in the
UK. UKCISA (UK Council for International Student Affairs)
and the **NUS (National Union of Students)** have both worked
with Endsleigh Insurance on policies designed specifically
for students' requirements, although there is a range of
other insurance providers you can use. Use a comparison
website such as www.moneysupermarket.com to compare
prices and cover.

Travel insurance

For your journey from your home country and any trips you take
outside the UK, it is advisable to take out travel insurance. You
will need to protect yourself and your belongings from
any mishaps, accidents or illness along the way. Check your
health insurance, to see whether your policy covers you while
you travel.

Contents insurance

Although the risk of being a victim of crime remains low, student accommodation can be a target for thieves as it often contains portable technology like laptops, MP3 players and mobile phones. Contents insurance is designed to cover the value of possessions in your student accommodation. If you are living in university accommodation, check whether contents insurance is included in your rent. You will need to take out your own insurance in private, rented accommodation.

Health insurance

If you are not entitled to treatment by the National Health Service (see p.195 for more on health), you should take out your own health insurance to cover the costs of any treatment and additional costs incurred as a result of illness. Even if you are covered, you may have to wait for certain NHS services, so insurance may give you the benefit of quicker treatment. You may be able to extend any health insurance policy covering you in your home country.

> **"** If you have any serious medical conditions, it's probably worth looking at what you would need from the NHS and the cost of private care if it becomes necessary. **"**
>
> *Alexandra Kamins, US*

Bills

You need to consider the cost of bills when budgeting and when deciding on the most suitable accommodation. Check whether any bills or services are included in your rental payments. Students in halls of residence will find that many of these bills are already included within their costs. Examples of monthly costs provided here have been calculated by dividing annual costs by 12 between four students. You will need to calculate figures according to costs payable locally, considering the number of students and the length of time for which you will be responsible for bills in your accommodation.

Gas and electricity

According to figures from the Department of Energy and Climate Change, the average annual domestic electricity bill in the UK in 2011 was £434. The average annual domestic gas bill for the same year was £697. If you share a house with three other people, you could be looking at bills of around £9 per month for electricity and £14.50 per month for gas. These amounts will vary depending on where you live, the supplier you use, the appliances and heating system that you have and how much you use them. In these examples from the Department of Energy and Climate Change, bills were paid using **direct debit**, which is automatically deducted from your bank account. Direct debit is normally cheaper than using a payment plan or pre-payment card, although pre-payment may make budgeting and controlling what you spend easier.

Water

Water rates vary according to where you live in the country and whether you are on a water meter or paying water bills. If using a meter, you are charged for the amount that you use, so it pays to be economical with your water usage. You would be looking at estimated average bills of around £376 per year in 2012–13. This works out at around £7.80 per month if sharing with three other people and if payment is divided over the full 12-month period. In some regions the yearly cost can be over £500. This is based on figures from Ofwat, the economic regulator of the water industry in England and Wales. Scottish bills remain just below average. Customers in Northern Ireland pay a similar amount.

Council Tax or rates

These payments are for local services including the police, fire brigade and rubbish collection. If you live in halls of residence, or if everyone in your shared accommodation is a full-time student, you'll be exempt from paying Council Tax in England, Scotland and Wales (and exempt from paying rates in Northern Ireland). Even if you share with someone who's not a full-time student, you could still be entitled to a discount.

TV licence

Anyone who owns a TV in the UK pays a licence fee of around £145 per year. If you watch or record live TV using devices such as laptops, mobile phones or consoles, you will also need to purchase a licence. If you share private accommodation, one licence can be shared between housemates, although self-contained accommodation will require the purchase of an individual licence. Check www.tvlicensing.co.uk for further details of whether you will need a licence. Costs can be paid by direct debit.

Phone and internet

There is a lot of choice when deciding on a phone and internet provider. Internet service provider choice may be restricted by local availability. Some providers require a British Telecom (BT) phone line to be in place beforehand, while providers that use fibre optic cables are only available in certain areas. Cheapest broadband deals start from just a few pounds per month.

In order to use a mobile (or cell phone) in the UK, think about buying a UK SIM card while you are here. You may find it cheaper to take out a mobile phone on a contract basis rather than using pay-as-you-go, although a lack of UK credit history may prevent this when you first arrive or if you are only in the UK for a short time. Shop around for the best deal using a price comparison website such as www.moneysupermarket.com. Prices range from a few pounds a month for SIM-card-only deals.

Other living expenses

Transport

There are discount and saver cards for students on local transport. It works out cheaper to buy a weekly, monthly or even termly pass if you know you will be using public transport regularly. Of course the cheapest option is to walk, if you don't have far to go, while cycling may work out cheaper than public transport in the long term. Get advice from your institution about local transport costs.

For travel across the UK and outside the country, it is often more cost effective to buy in advance, although there may be some last-minute deals available too.

Shopping

Supermarkets are cheaper than small, local shops, with the larger stores selling everything from food to clothing, home and electrical items. However, in some areas, large supermarkets can be tricky to get to without a car. Buying in large amounts works out cheaper than shopping for an individual, so sharing food shopping with fellow students can be more economical. Look out for special offers too. The website www.mysupermarket.co.uk allows you to check prices and get a sense of costs and to find the cheapest deals when you arrive in the UK.

Try local indoor or outdoor markets, which can be very reasonable for a range of items, including meat, fish, and fruit and vegetables. For clothing and items for the home, you can get some great bargains through second-hand shops, charity shops, markets and eBay.

> **❝** London is pretty expensive when it comes to living costs. I have friends living in other parts of the UK who can survive on less than £50 per week. **❞**
>
> *Cynthia Cheah, Malaysia*

Eating out

It is cheaper to eat at home (or to take a **packed lunch**), but eating out can be a good way to socialise, and there are bargains to be had. University canteens and cafes may offer subsidised meals at a reasonable price. At other establishments, there may be special offers, particularly at quieter times of the week. Look out for 'early bird' offers (for those eating early in the evening), midweek specials and lunchtime menus. You can sometimes get two or three courses for a fixed price. Pubs and cafes tend to be cheaper than restaurants. The price of alcoholic drinks can bump up the price of eating out in restaurants; some restaurants, particularly in cities, allow you to bring your own wine, thereby reducing the cost. Look out for signs saying BYO or 'bring your own'.

Free time

There are so many ways to spend your free time in the UK: eating out, pubs and nightclubs, concerts, theatres, museums, galleries, playing and watching sports, historical and heritage sites, parks, visiting the sea or the countryside. You can spend a lot of money on leisure activities, but there are many free and discounted activities available, including free museums and galleries and last-minute discounted theatre tickets. Ask at your local tourist information office for details, or browse online for free and discounted activities in your area.

Costs of study

Don't forget to factor in the costs associated with studying, as these can be substantial. Your university and college will provide you with a list of items; check which of these are essential. Books can be expensive, although copies should be available to use free of charge in the institution's library and you may be able to buy second-hand. You will need to do a certain amount of printing and copying and will need stationery. Most institutions have their own reasonably priced shops for stationery and basic equipment. Field trips and visits may be an essential part of your course. Some universities charge college fees, while postgraduate students may be expected to pay research support fees or bench fees. Clarify all these extra costs in advance so you can be financially prepared.

According to the 2010 *NUS Services Student Lifestyle Report*, students surveyed spent on average £263.21 per term on the costs of study. An average of £75.86 was spent on buying books, £63.76 on course excursions and £50 on other costs.

Tips for surviving on a budget

Set a budget

Make a note of all the money going into your account and all the money going out every week to work out how much you have left to spend. Use the UNIAID student calculator (www.studentcalculator.org.uk/international) to set a budget and then make sure you stick to it.

Follow these tips to help you stick to your budget.

- Plan your meals for the week.
- Make a list and only buy what you need.

- Check use-by dates so you don't end up wasting food.
- Don't go shopping when you're hungry.
- Don't just buy branded products; supermarket own-brand items can be just as good.
- Look out for discount supermarkets such as Aldi and Lidl.
- Items that won't go off can be bought in bulk.
- Shop just before stores close to get discounted food.
- Prepare a packed lunch to take to college or university, instead of buying it there.
- Ask around for the cheapest places to buy clothes, stationery and things for the home.
- Use markets, second-hand shops, car boot sales and eBay.
- Look out for second-hand student books on university notice boards.

Discounts

Always take advantage of the following discounts.

- Use your National Union of Students (NUS) card.
- Get an **International Student Identity Card** (**ISIC**) if travelling overseas.
- Always ask about student discounts in shops, restaurants, cinemas, for sport, travel and so on.
- Look out for discount vouchers.
- Use reward cards to gain savings over the longer term.
- Use sports facilities at your college or university.
- Use moneysavingexpert.com for further tips.

Things you can do for free

One of the best ways of making your money stretch further is by doing things that don't cost anything at all.

- Walk instead of taking public transport.
- Take advantage of free entry to many museums and galleries.
- Visit local parks.
- Explore the area where you live.
- Use Skype or webcams to contact friends and family.
- Join a local online community such as Freecycle for free items that people are getting rid of.
- Volunteer (just check your visa or entry clearance conditions first).

STUDENT STORY
Cynthia Cheah, Malaysia

Cynthia Cheah from Penang in Malaysia is currently studying for an MSc in Organisational Behaviour at Goldsmiths, University of London.

She ended up in London for a number of reasons. "I wanted to experience a culture that is different from where I come from, but I also prefer to be in the city. The education system in the UK is pretty similar to Malaysia, because Malaysia was once ruled by the British, so this made it easier for me to adapt."

Cynthia considered a number of criteria when deciding where in the UK to study, including location, subjects and lecturers, methods of assessment and employability after the course. "I had decided on the course I wanted to do before picking the right university. However, the subjects offered influenced my choice when picking the right course at the right institution."

She chose to use the support of an agent when making her application and speaks favourably about the support she received. "I would highly recommend it because it makes the whole process easier. The agency provided all the necessary forms for me to fill in and they sent it over for me. The longest part was waiting for a reply about my application. Once I got my offer letter, everything moved pretty fast."

When she came to apply for a visa, she used the agent's services once again. "Having an agent really helped because everything was arranged by them. My only responsibility was to fill in the form and hand it in personally. No interviews or anything. It took around three days to get my approved visa."

Cynthia felt well supported by her university too, even before she arrived in the UK. "The university was able to provide me with all the information I needed including accommodation, course information, how to prepare and survival tips. The international student department in my university was really helpful and replied to my emails within 24 hours (which is very efficient, in my opinion)."

When she arrived, Cynthia got involved in the international week activities which helped her to adapt to UK life. "It was a good chance to expose myself to some of the culture here and to meet new friends."

So what has she discovered about the UK during her time living and studying here? "Other than the weather, I've had no problem adjusting to life in the UK at all. It rains too much in London! But I don't think it is hard to adjust to life in London because it is so diverse here."

"In the cities, everyone walks really fast. That says a lot about their lifestyle! Time management is really important. The motto, 'work hard, play hard' kind of describes the lifestyle here. They work hard during the day and play hard at night and during the weekends (at least that's what I think). My friends told me the British are grumpy and unhelpful, but throughout my stay here, all I've met are friendly and really helpful people."

She prefers the convenience of living in university halls, but also has some tips about renting.

"Rents in London are pretty expensive (for halls and private properties). One tip for potential students is to never trust the pictures uploaded on websites when looking for accommodation. They never reflect the true condition of the place."

Cynthia finds that it is always cheaper to cook than to eat out, but has discovered a range of food on offer in London. "Another benefit of living in London is the diversity, even when it comes to food. So, it doesn't matter which part of the world you are from, you can probably find a restaurant that serves food from your home country. The food portions are huge here! But make sure you stock up on familiar food from home before you come here, because it is one of the best remedies for home sickness."

"London is pretty expensive when it comes to living costs. I have friends living in other parts of the UK who can survive on less than £50 per week." Luckily, Cynthia knows all the ways to find the best deals. "There are a lot of benefits for students. Remember to look out for all the notices for student discounts in restaurants and shops, and always bring your NUS student card with you; it helps save a lot of money."

Cynthia has struggled to find work while she studies. "I have found it really hard to get a part time job here without any connections. I think networking is very important when it comes to job hunting. A local friend once told me, 'Be ready to talk to anyone, wherever you are on the train or in a queue, because you never know which one of them might be your future boss.' Good advice, indeed!"

She has taken the time to explore the rest of the country. "It is really convenient to travel in the UK by train. It's not expensive when you book early and with a student travel card. It is also pretty easy to book cheap accommodation as long as you are willing to spend some time searching. There are a lot of hidden gems in the UK, especially in the countryside and small towns."

Cynthia has also taken advantage of the UK's proximity to the rest of Europe. "With so many different airlines that offer flights to different EU countries, travelling to Europe from the UK can be pretty cheap (again, the internet is the best place to look for cheap deals). It is easy for me because I don't need a visa to travel within the EU, but for students that need one, I suggest you apply early – you might not be able to get an appointment near the holidays as it gets busy."

Although her experiences in the UK have been mainly positive, there have been some negative incidents for Cynthia. "I've had one or two negative experiences with racism, but it was very minor. I once ignored a group of students at a party and they started making jokes about us because they thought we couldn't understand them; they apologised afterwards when they realised their mistake. My only advice is to never take those comments seriously."

So, what is next for Cynthia when her course comes to an end? "Now that applications for the post-study work visa have closed, it is going to be harder to remain here after my studies. This is mainly because it is hard for international students to get a job. A lot of companies prefer to hire locals or EU citizens because it is easier for them." She suggests starting early with the search for work. "You shouldn't start looking for a job after you've completed your course. And remember to network as much as you can!"

She has some good advice for students who are thinking of studying in the UK. "Never be afraid to ask questions. It can be a big move to come to the UK to study, so always ask around (friends who've been here, university student services departments and so on). Come with an open heart and be curious about everything (well, most things) and you will enjoy it. Also, be prepared to step out of your comfort zone!"

"The experience itself is the best thing about studying in the UK – living a life different from the one back home, exploring a different world and learning about the cultures and lifestyle."

Gower College

Gower College Swansea is one of the largest further education providers in Wales, offering over 45 A level subjects in the areas of Arts, Languages, Humanities, Science, Technology, Engineering and Maths. Other courses include a full range of vocational programmes, HNCs/HNDs and pre-University Foundation programmes, which give students the opportunity to progress either into higher education or gain skills to enter into the global employment market.

Most students progress to higher education, studying at universities and specialist colleges throughout the UK. Last year nine of our students were successful in their applications to the prestigious universities of Oxford and Cambridge.

A waterfront city and the regional capital of South West Wales, Swansea is a modern, thriving city very near to the Gower Peninsula – an Area of Outstanding Natural Beauty – with 32 miles of coastline, award winning golden beaches and lush, rolling countryside.

Swansea boasts excellent sporting facilities, including the Wales National Pool and Liberty Stadium, a 20,000-seat venue which is home to Barclays Premier League club Swansea City FC and the Ospreys rugby team.

Just one hour from Cardiff International airport and with good road and rail links to London, Swansea is one of the safest and cheapest cities to live in the UK.

Student testimonials

" *As an international student I have been welcomed fully by the college and my language skills have improved enormously thanks to the support I have received here.* **"**

Monjurul, Bangladesh

❝ *Living in Swansea is very safe, convenient and not too expensive. I especially enjoy the sea views and spending my free time on the beachfront. In the future I hope to study a degree in business and would certainly recommend the A level programme to students who are looking for a good quality education in a vibrant, friendly city.* **❞**

Nhung, Vietnam

Chapter 12
Life in the UK

It is important to prepare yourself for life in the UK. The transition is likely to be easier if you know what to expect: what the food and the weather will be like, how to open a bank account, your options for travel and bringing your family, as well as health, working and staying safe. Unfortunately, sometimes things do go wrong, so this chapter also includes information on how to tackle problems you may encounter with your educational experience.

For most students, their UK education experience is positive and life-changing. Learning what life is like in the UK should help you to anticipate the differences and help you to make the most of your time here.

Food

The UK has not been traditionally renowned for its food, but over the last decade or two, things have been steadily improving. Many students come here with worries about what they will eat and whether they will like the food. Perhaps you have heard of British fish and chips or bangers and mash (sausages and mashed potato), but there is a much broader range of food available! Restaurants showing the influence of cuisine from India, China and Europe can be seen in most towns, with wider choices from across the world available in larger cities. Many larger towns and cities will have supermarkets specialising in food from particular countries, where you will be able to buy the foods that remind you of home.

> **❝** I had heard a lot of rumours about British cooking, but thankfully most of them turned out not to be true. Thanks to the Commonwealth there are a lot of different restaurants and cuisines available. Though it is still hard finding proper European-style bread. **❞**
>
> *David Stoll, Luxembourg*

> **❝** The taste of the food is relative; it depends on your previous diet. I come from Indonesia where we use a lot of spices in our meals, so using only salt and pepper is kind of bland for me. If you do miss home-cooked food, just go to the city and you may find stores that sell the ingredients you need. Be creative, because staying abroad is the best way to learn how to cook by yourself. **❞**
>
> *Nadya Pramudita, Indonesia*

> **❝** At first the food situation was stressful for me – there are a lot of items I would consider common in the US that are not available here. However, as with all things, I became more comfortable with the food available. **❞**
>
> *Kimberly Stevenson, US*

Vegetarianism is acceptable across the UK, with many cafes and restaurants catering for vegetarians, sometimes for vegans, and also for certain food intolerances. Some eating places will offer a halal menu. If you have special dietary requirements and want to eat out, it is useful to discuss your needs with the staff beforehand.

Breakfast

In the UK, a traditional breakfast consists of bacon, eggs, tomatoes, mushrooms and sausages washed down with a mug of tea. Each region has different variations on the full English (or Scottish, Welsh or Irish) breakfast; you might also see it called a fry-up or all-day breakfast. Most households don't cook this every morning and a breakfast of cereal or toast is more common, eaten sometime between 6am and 9am.

Lunch

Lunch tends to be a light meal eaten between 12pm and 2pm, maybe sandwiches, a salad or soup. To save money or to meet specific dietary requirements, you can prepare a packed lunch to take to college or university. You can normally expect a break from work or study of 30 minutes to an hour at lunchtimes.

Dinner

The evening meal may be called tea, dinner or supper. It is often the largest meal of the day and can be eaten any time from around 5pm. British households eat a range of foods; perhaps meat and two veg (meat, potatoes, vegetables and gravy) or shepherd's pie (a dish made of lamb with a mashed potato topping), as well as a whole host of other options. People in the UK eat a lot of potatoes, but these days rice and pasta dishes from around the world are just as likely to be eaten as a traditional British dish. Some families will have a starter or dessert. On

Sundays, British families may have a traditional roast dinner of beef, lamb, pork or chicken served with vegetables, Yorkshire pudding, stuffing, gravy and a range of sauces.

Weather

> **"** I always tell students to be prepared for the weather – chilly and mostly grey. It may seem silly, but it is true that the weather can have a negative effect on people, especially our students who come from colourful, warm places like Sri Lanka or Thailand. It's a real shock to them, and I do honestly want them to be prepared. I come from Texas (also colourful and warm) and the weather has been a major source of irritation for me!" **"**
>
> *International officer*

The weather in the UK can be changeable. Although there aren't huge variations in climate, the north tends to be colder than the south, with much of the west wetter than the east. Clothes that can be layered will probably be more useful than clothing for extremes of temperature. Warm clothes will be needed any time from October to March, while wet weather gear like raincoats and umbrellas can be useful at any time of the year. Summer is generally warm, requiring lighter clothing and footwear. Nearly all houses in the UK have central heating systems, so you should be warm enough indoors.

A tolerant society

The UK is known for its diversity, tolerance and respect, and discriminatory behaviour is not acceptable. Any issues of intolerance that you encounter based on race, religion, gender, sexuality, age or disability can be discussed with your international office, which will be able to advise you what to do.

> ❝ It's important to come with an open mind and to be prepared for a change. ❞
>
> *International officer*

Health

Although the UK is known for its National Health Service (NHS), you shouldn't assume that you will automatically get free treatment. Students from the EEA and any country with reciprocal health arrangements will qualify for free treatment through the NHS. International students on a full-time course lasting six months or more (or a course of any length if substantially funded by the UK government) will be entitled to free treatment in England, Wales and Northern Ireland. International full-time students in Scotland will get free treatment regardless of the length of their course.

The Department of Health website – www.dh.gov.uk – has useful information on whether you qualify for free treatment. All eligible students should register with a local doctor shortly after arrival; your institution will show you how. For those with an on-going medical condition, bring a translated copy of a doctor's report outlining your condition, treatment and medication required. Check with your local British embassy or high commission for any vaccinations needed for entry to the UK. It is useful to carry a health certificate listing your vaccinations.

Free treatment on the NHS includes visiting a GP and both emergency and non-emergency hospital treatment. There are charges for other services from the NHS: prescribed medicines, dental treatment and optical treatment. Most medicines, except for basic remedies, need to be prescribed by a doctor and then prepared at a pharmacy. These prescriptions currently cost £7.65 in England but are free in Scotland, Wales and Northern Ireland. Full-time students aged under 19 should be exempt from prescription charges. Some adults may also be exempt, for example if you are pregnant or on a low income. See the UKCISA information sheet, *Keeping Healthy*, for more details.

EU students should bring a **European Health Insurance Card** (**EHIC**) from their home country.

Dental treatment

It can be difficult to register as an NHS patient for dental treatment in certain areas, as some dentists are too full to accept new patients. Your institution can tell you about the situation in your area. Charges are made for all dental treatments, whether NHS or private, but are lower for NHS treatment. Go for a dental examination before you come to the UK and make sure you have adequate insurance if you are studying here for less than six months, as you will not be able to register as an NHS patient.

Eye tests

You can take an eye test for around £25 to £30 at a high street ophthalmic optician. If you need to buy glasses (spectacles) or contact lenses, ask your optician for the details of your eye prescription. It is worth shopping around and you may find cheaper deals elsewhere or online.

Health insurance

Any students who are not eligible for free NHS treatment
will need to take out health insurance to cover their costs.
A small number of critical NHS services are free to all, including
some emergency medical treatment, family planning services,
treatment for some communicable diseases and compulsory
psychiatric treatment. It is essential to be covered for all other
medical expenses.

Keeping in touch

When you're a long way from home, being able to keep in touch
with friends and family is really important. Long-distance calls
can cost a fortune, so look around for the best value ways to
contact your nearest and dearest.

Online

University and college students will get free access to the internet
through the institution's network, enabling free email on campus
and in halls of residence. Other options like webcams, instant
messaging and Vonage or Skype are free ways to keep in touch;
check the conditions to get free messaging through Vonage and
Skype, as they do charge for some services.

Telephone

If you prefer to phone, you can choose from public payphones,
private landlines or mobile phones. Public payphones are
available, although there are fewer now as most people have
mobiles. You can pay with coins, but also with phone cards and
credit and debit cards. It can be more costly to call long distance
from a payphone.

To get cheap overseas calls, use a pre-dial provider such as www. phonecheap.co.uk, www.abroadcall.co.uk or www.telediscount. co.uk. There's no need to set up a special account – you simply dial a prefix number before your call to get the discounted rate, ranging from around 1p per minute. Try to use a landline for your calls, as mobile and payphone calls can be more expensive with some providers. You can also buy international phone cards that offer a lower rate than a regular call from a landline.

 It is polite to queue when waiting for a service. In fact, the British are known for it. 99

International officer

If you are using someone's private telephone line, perhaps belonging to your homestay host, it is polite to agree telephone usage in advance. If they will be charged for the calls you are making, then you should pay for them. You can ask to reverse the charges, where the person receiving the call pays, but this can be pricy. To do so, dial 155 for the UK international operator and ask for a reversed charge call.

If you are renting a property and take out a contract for a landline in the UK, check whether the provider offers an international calling package as these offer cheaper calls. Phone calls from landlines within the UK tend to be cheaper after 6pm, before 8am and at weekends. International calls are often cheaper after 8pm and before 8am.

Different towns and areas of the UK have their own area codes; for example, 0161 for Manchester and 028 for Belfast. Use the phone directory to find out dialling codes for the UK and overseas at www.thephonebook.bt.com. UK mobile numbers start with 07. Local rate numbers, often used by businesses, start with 0800, 0844, 0845, 0870 and 0871. Although these are free or charged at local rate from a landline, they cost more from a mobile.

Mobile phones

You can use your mobile phone in the UK; check with your provider back home how much you will be charged for using it in the UK. Bear in mind that international calls can be costly. It might work out cheaper to buy a SIM card here, particularly one that specialises in good international rates. You can opt for pay-as-you-go where you pay for the calls that you make; you can manage your spending easily this way, although call costs are a little more expensive. Alternatively, opt for a contract where you pay a monthly tariff that may include free minutes and texts (SMS). These tend to offer cheaper calls, but it can be easy to build up a large bill. In addition, many contracts require you to have some UK credit history and may last for a minimum of 12 months, which can be tricky for some international students.

Post

The UK has a reliable postal service, with first-class UK-bound mail normally arriving in a day or two and cheaper second-class mail taking a little longer. Postage times to other countries vary. You will find red post boxes throughout towns and residential areas; you can also use the Post Office, particularly if you need to post larger items. Post Office staff will weigh your parcel and tell you how much it will cost to send. At the Post Office you can order foreign currency or traveller's cheques and transfer money.

Smoking is banned in all indoor public spaces (and some outdoor spaces, such as football grounds and railway platforms) across the UK.

Staying safe

It is normal for international students to feel vulnerable when they first arrive in a new country or city. You are more at risk when you don't know an area or the local perspective on what is safe behaviour. Colleges and institutions are aware of this and are conscious of the need to support you to stay safe. They might provide you with a leaflet about looking after yourself or arrange an information session when you first arrive. The UK is a relatively safe country with low levels of crime; most international students have a safe and enjoyable time here by staying aware of their safety and following a few simple guidelines.

Police in the UK are here to help and protect the general public. You can approach a police officer or contact a local police station with worries about crime or to report an incident.

In an emergency, if a life is in danger or if a crime is in progress, you can call for help for free by dialling 999. You will be asked which service you require (police, fire service or ambulance) before being asked to explain the details of the emergency. Do not use this number for non-urgent matters.

Legal requirements

You may have to register your stay in the UK with the local police, if your passport has been stamped accordingly. Institutions with many international students may arrange for the police to come to the college or university. If not, you'll need to go to a police station within seven days of arrival, taking with you your passport, two passport-sized photographs, a

confirmation letter from your institution, proof of address
and the registration fee (currently £34). There may be limited
opening hours, you may be able to register at only one police
station in the area or you may need to book an appointment; find
out more from your college or university.

Students based in London and covered by the Metropolitan Police
should attend the Overseas Visitors Records Office (the details
are below), ideally early in the morning, since it can get very
busy. Passport photos are not required, as they will take your
photograph as part of the registration process. Check opening
hours at www.met.police.uk/overseas_visitors_records_office.

Overseas Visitors Records Office
Brandon House
Ground Floor
180 Borough High Street
London SE1 1LH
Tel: 020 7230 1208

If your details change or you leave the area, you will need to
notify the police or records office of the changes.

It is essential to be aware of legal restrictions around drink and
drugs in the UK. You must be 18 or over to drink alcohol in
public or buy it. It is against the law to drink alcohol and drive.
It is a criminal offence to be in possession of or to sell drugs
(heroin, cocaine, ecstasy, LSD, cannabis and so on). You should
not carry weapons including guns, imitation guns, knives or
pepper spray.

> Minami Eto was surprised to discover how quiet the city centre could be on weekday evenings compared with Japan.
>
> I was surprised. At home it is really busy and crowded, so I felt a little bit scared. **99**
>
> *Minami Eto, Japan*

Tips for personal safety

- Don't walk alone late at night; stay in a group or use public transport.
- Find out whether there are local areas that aren't safe.
- Keep someone informed of your plans.
- Take care of your friends.
- Don't accept lifts from strangers.
- Don't hitchhike.
- If using taxis, check that they have a registered photo ID card inside and a taxi licence plate.
- In pubs and clubs, keep your drink with you.

Facing trouble

- If you think there may be trouble, avoid it by crossing the street or walking away.
- You can't reason with someone who is drunk; it is best to walk away.
- If someone tries to take your property by force, let them have it; property can be replaced.
- If you are attacked, shout or scream and run towards a populated area.
- Use a personal attack alarm.

Looking after your property

- Lock doors and windows when you go out.
- Don't let non-residents into your student accommodation.

- Keep valuables out of sight in your accommodation.
- Keep valuables out of sight when carrying them.
- Keep your bag closed and fastened.
- Try to avoid carrying large amounts of money.

 There were a surprising number of scams and fake accommodation offers online.

Alexandra Kamins, US

Watch out for scams

- If it sounds too good to be true, it probably is.
- Don't give out bank or personal details.
- Don't give cash to strangers.
- Don't send money for accommodation that you haven't visited.
- Genuine scholarship organisations will not ask you for fees or bank details.
- Stay aware and be suspicious.

Remember that most students will not be affected by crime, but awareness of the risks will help you to stay safe and enjoy your time in the UK.

Banks and money

You are going to need a bank account fairly soon when you get here. Since it's not recommended to bring large amounts of cash with you, you will need your account up and running quickly so you can access your money.

Opening an account

It can be a bit of a challenge to get a bank account opened. Banks in the UK normally need proof of who you are and proof of where you live. The rules about what they will and won't accept as evidence varies between banks and can change. Talk to your university or college; while they probably won't recommend a bank to you, they will have the experience to know which banks are convenient and the simplest for international students to join. Some universities will even bring bank representatives in to meet you. Although it's tempting to open an account with the first bank you see, check out what is on offer and how they compare with one another first. The charges for international services will vary.

To open an account you will need:

- your passport
- your visa
- a letter from your college or university.

International students tend to be offered a basic account, allowing access to money through a cashpoint or ATM and the ability to set up standing orders and direct debits to pay bills, but no credit or overdraft facilities. Once you have opened an account it can take up to a week to get your bank card sent through. Your PIN number will be sent separately; you need both PIN and card to get money out of an ATM. Check how you can withdraw money before you receive these.

Transferring money

Think about how you are going to move money from your home country to your UK bank account. The different methods vary widely in the time they take and the cost incurred. Whenever you are changing currency, you are going to have to pay for the privilege. Spend a bit of time working out which methods suit you best and think ahead to save yourself money. Keep any paperwork when transferring money, in case of discrepancies or problems.

Bank transfers are quick, taking only a few working days. Make sure that your home bank has the facilities to make international transfers. Once you have opened your UK account, you can make contact with your home bank. Remember to bring your home bank contact and account details with you. Check how much they will charge for transfers.

A banker's draft can be brought with you from your home bank and used as funds to open a bank account in the UK. If it is in sterling (GBP) currency, it will be quick to process and you shouldn't be charged, but bringing it in another currency will incur a charge and delay processing by a month or more. A personal cheque from your home country may also result in a charge and take just as long to clear. Traveller's cheques can be cashed at a bank or bureau de change or paid into your account in the UK; if they're not in sterling there will be a commission to pay. If your credit card is accepted in the UK, you could withdraw money and pay this into a bank account, not forgetting to check the cost. Of course, there are always money transfers through companies such as Western Union and MoneyGram; these can be particularly fast but are likely to be more expensive.

Insurance

You will need insurance during your time in the UK. Travel, contents and health insurance may be required, depending on your circumstances. See p.175 for further details.

Family

There are no restrictions that prevent EU students bringing family with them while they study. New visa restrictions mean that, for new visa applications, only postgraduate international students at universities (on courses at least 12 months long) and government-sponsored students will be able to bring their dependants. Postgraduate study refers to a course on the National Qualification Framework at level 7 or above (or level 11 in Scotland). Any adult dependants will be allowed to work.

If you are bringing children, you can talk to your local authority about finding a suitable school. Your children will need to attend school if you are here for more than a short stay. Most areas have information services about childcare provision for children under five, as well as on local groups and activities for parents. Children under 19 accompanying their student parents will be given home status, so you should be able to gain access to mainstream education for children aged 5 to 18 for free. There are some charges for early years education for children aged three and over; childcare for under threes has to be paid for.

If you are an international student on a course of six months or longer (or a course of any length that is UK government funded) and your husband or wife is living in the UK with you, they will be entitled to some free NHS treatment. The same applies to your children aged 16 or under (or up to 19 if they are in full-time education). In Scotland, treatment is available to full-time students and their dependants, regardless of the length of study.

You will need to investigate accommodation options as soon as you can. As affordable student housing is limited in the UK, you will find that affordable student family housing is particularly rare. There will be more choice in private, rented accommodation. International students requiring a visa will need to make arrangements for accommodation before arriving with a family; UK Border Agency immigration officials may decline you and your family entry to the UK without proof of accommodation.

Remember that your dependants will face the same challenges as you when adjusting to the UK, but without necessarily having the same systems of support in place. Encouraging them to get involved in activities and opportunities for learning may help to ease this process.

Travel

Driving

If you want to drive any vehicle in the UK, including a motorbike or moped, it is your responsibility to check out all the legal requirements. UKCISA has a useful information sheet on its website explaining whether your driving licence will be valid in the UK. Any vehicle must be insured, with road tax, registration documents and a valid MOT (to show that it is safe and roadworthy if it is over three years old). You will need to know and understand the rules of the Highway Code, which can be found at www.direct. gov.uk/en/TravelAndTransport/Highwaycode/index.htm.

Driving a car in a congested city like London is a challenge; the congestion charge and the difficulty of parking add to the impracticality. You may find alternative methods of getting about to be more suitable.

Cycling

Cycling is a cheap, healthy and green way to travel. Many towns and campuses are well equipped for cyclists, with good cycling paths and facilities for cyclists. You can expect to cycle around 5 miles in 30 minutes, so a bike might prove to be a better (and cheaper) option than public transport. Some universities run bike loan schemes to encourage two-wheeled travel.

Here are a few points to consider before you decide on cycling.

- Make sure there is somewhere you can store your bike securely; student bikes can be a target for thieves.
- Invest in a good-quality lock and check your insurance policy.
- Consider your safety: wear a helmet and visible clothing and familiarise yourself with the Highway Code.

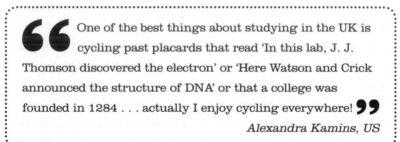

> One of the best things about studying in the UK is cycling past placards that read 'In this lab, J. J. Thomson discovered the electron' or 'Here Watson and Crick announced the structure of DNA' or that a college was founded in 1284 . . . actually I enjoy cycling everywhere!
>
> *Alexandra Kamins, US*

Public transport

The UK has a comprehensive network of public transport, with rail and coach services linking all parts of the UK. Local transport is built around the underground in London and bus, tram or train elsewhere. Travel costs can add up, so it is worth taking advice on how to get the cheapest fares.

Close proximity to mainland Europe means that you may also get the chance to explore other parts of the continent while you are here.

Local travel

Find out about your local bus, tram or underground service.
Weekly or termly passes are usually better value than individual
tickets. Get an Oyster card (travel smartcard) for travel across
London. If you can be flexible about when you need to attend
university, travelling off-peak is cheaper. Your college or
university will be able to tell you about travel in your local area,
including discounts available. On buses in some towns you will
need to pay with the exact money.

Travel within the UK

You can cross the country by train or coach; long-distance trains
are often the faster option with more comfort and facilities,
but you will pay more. Look out for sales and special offers on
selected train and coach routes.

For the cheapest train tickets, book in advance, from about
12 weeks ahead. It can be surprising to find that two singles
can sometimes end up cheaper than a return. Use a 'best fare
finder' option if you are flexible about travel times and want
to search according to price. A single ticket from London to
Edinburgh can be well in excess of £100, but you can find
tickets for as little as £18.50 if you can travel at unpopular or
unsociable hours.

Try www.thetrainline.com to search for train tickets. As an
alternative, Megatrain (http://megatrain.com) offers cheap fares
on regular trains.

You can buy a 16–25 Railcard (www.16-25railcard.co.uk) for
£28 a year (£65 for three years); it will save you one-third off
rail fares. If you're aged 16 to 25, or over 26 and in full-time
education, you're eligible to apply.

If you plan to travel by coach, a Young Persons Coachcard (www.
nationalexpress.com/coach/Offers/StudentCoachDeals.cfm)
costing £10 can save you 30% off tickets. It is aimed at 16 to
26 year olds and all full-time students. National Express also
offers Funfare tickets online, which offer the lowest prices up to
three months in advance.

Megabus offers cheap fares between cities in the UK. There are
some restrictions, much like budget airlines. You can only book
tickets before you travel, they often use alternative bus depots,
you have limited luggage allowance and you can't take hot foods
or drinks on board. They can be one of the cheapest ways to get
across the country; find out more at http://uk.megabus.com.

> **"** My advice would be to get a Young Person's
> Railcard (16–25 Railcard) and make good use of
> Funfare coach tickets (the lowest price tickets from
> National Express). **"**
>
> *Yana Dautova, Russia*

Take a look at www.translink.co.uk for details of travel in
Northern Ireland. If you need to travel from Northern Ireland
to the rest of the UK, you will need to investigate ferry and air
travel. Eurolines offers combined coach and ferry tickets to
Northern Ireland at www.eurolines.co.uk. You can buy combined
rail and ferry tickets too; try www.raileasy.co.uk for details. For
the best prices on flights, try www.skyscanner.net, searching
across the whole month to find the cheapest deals.

International travel

Take out an International Student Identity Card (ISIC) at www.
isiccard.com to extend your student discounts to other countries
and save money on travel and accommodation.

> You may need a visa to visit countries outside the UK. Some
> countries may also require three or six months to be left on
> your UK student visa, which can cause problems if you wish
> to travel at the end of your studies. Check before you make
> travel plans.

As with travel within the UK, try to plan ahead and book early.
You may still find some last-minute deals too. Use comparison
sites such as www.skyscanner.net, www.kayak.com or www.
travelsupermarket.com to check out the cheapest flights. Try
www.eurolines.co.uk for scheduled coach travel across Europe.
European railcards such as InterRail and Eurail can be a great
saving, making budgeting easier. Try www.interrailnet.com and
www.eurail.com for fixed-price travel by rail across a range of
countries. Take a look at www.ferrysavers.co.uk for deals by
sea; if you fancy travelling to Europe under the sea, go to
www.eurotunnel.com.

Some travel organisations specialise in student or backpacker
travel and offer expertise and specialist deals. Try somewhere
like STA Travel (www.statravel.co.uk) if you prefer the support of
planning with a travel agency.

Accommodation while travelling

The Youth Hostel Association (YHA) offers a range of reasonably
priced accommodation across England and Wales, with maximum
stays of a week or two. SYHA (Hostelling Scotland) and HINI
(Hostelling International Northern Ireland) offer similar

provision in Scotland and Northern Ireland respectively. You will need to join and pay membership fees if you want to stay here. Membership may be useful if you want to look at budget ways of travelling around the UK or Europe during your holidays. You can join Hostelling International in your home country to gain access to hostels in the UK. For more information, see www. hihostels.com.

You may find that independent hostels and budget hotels are also very good value. Try searching at www.hostelbookers.com and www.hostelworld.com. Hostels may offer private rooms as well as shared dormitory accommodation. Find out what is included and what you'll have to pay extra for to help decide on your best option.

If you're feeling braver and looking for free accommodation, you could look at a hospitality network such as www.couchsurfing. org or www.hospitalityclub.org. You shouldn't have to pay anything for your accommodation but you may be asked to contribute by cooking a meal or helping out. Make sure you follow all the safety tips in order to have a safe and positive experience.

Working and volunteering

Working or volunteering in the UK can help to enhance your employability, looks great on a CV and helps to improve your language. On the other hand, too much work can have a negative effect on your studies, put you in breach of immigration conditions and leave you exhausted. It is all about following the rules and finding the right balance.

> **❝** I did voluntary placements which came in very handy when applying for jobs later. My advice would be to do some work while at university; it can do wonders for your CV. **❞**
>
> *Yana Dautova, Russia*

Working

EU students can work in the UK. As a general rule, most universities advise their students to work no more than 10 to 15 hours per week in term time. Working more than this may start to affect your studies, and your studies are the purpose of being here, after all.

Restrictions for students on a Tier 4 visa vary according to where you study. Students at universities on courses at QCF level 6 (SCQF level 9) or over can work 20 hours per week in term time. If you study at a further education college, you can work 10 hours per week during term time. In both cases, you can also work full-time during the official university holidays. Students at private colleges and language schools have no right to work during their time in the UK. If you are coming to the UK for less than six months and intend to gain entry clearance on arrival as a Student Visitor, you will be unable to work or volunteer during your stay in the UK.

You should not rely on income from work to fund yourself through your studies, as there is no guarantee you will find a job; even if you do, the amount you earn is highly unlikely to fully cover your costs.

National Insurance number

When you get a job, you will need to obtain a **National Insurance number** (**NINo**). This is a personal reference number used for tax, National Insurance and the social security system. You can contact Jobcentre Plus on 0845 600 0643 to start the application process. Employers like to know that you have a NINo or have applied for one, as it often reassures them that you have the right to work.

If you work, you will have to pay income tax and National Insurance contributions. The amount of income tax payable depends on how much you earn; everyone has a personal allowance, on which no tax is paid. The personal allowance for the 2012–2013 tax year is £8,105, so you will not pay income tax on the first £8,105 you earn.

Volunteering

Volunteering in the UK involves unpaid work or activities, often for the benefit of the community. Students volunteer for many reasons: sometimes out of altruism, but often as a way to meet people, improve language skills and gain experience. Volunteers don't get paid, but sometimes get travel expenses or a meal while volunteering. Opportunities are many and varied, requiring differing commitments of time or of expertise. You will need to look at what is available, whether it will complement and fit around your studies, whether you can get there easily and so on. Most universities and colleges will have a team that has information on local volunteering opportunities.

Most employers and voluntary organisations will ask for references from someone in a position of responsibility, perhaps a previous employer or teacher. It is handy to bring contact details of these people with you (but check first that they would be happy to provide a reference). If a job or voluntary placement involves

working with children or vulnerable people, the organisation
will ask for a **Criminal Records Bureau** (**CRB**) or police check to
be carried out. If you have been living abroad, you may have to
provide a criminal record check (or good behaviour record) from
your home country. For further details visit www.direct.gov.uk/crb.

Religion

The UK offers religious tolerance, allowing people of all
denominations to practise their faith. Christianity is the major
religion, so you will see churches across the country, from rural
to metropolitan areas. Places of worship for other world religions
are available in cities, but less so in smaller towns and villages.
Colleges and universities may have their own places for prayer
and reflection and their own chaplain to represent all faiths
(and none). You may wish to ask questions about local places of
worship before you choose your institution. The staff will also be
able to talk to you about arrangements for religious observance,
religious holidays and the availability of halal or kosher foods.
A range of student societies are in place for faith groups,
particularly at universities; if your faith is not represented, you
may be able to set up a group.

What if things go wrong?

It would be nice to imagine that every international student
who comes to the UK has a fantastic experience and does well
academically; of course, that isn't always the case. Some students
do not fully prepare for and research what is on offer and
inevitably end up disappointed. No matter how well you prepare
and research beforehand, things don't always go as planned.
Students face a range of issues, from disliking
the course and not coping academically to homesickness
and illness. Others face financial problems and family crises.

Anticipating what some of those issues might be and considering how you will cope may help you to deal with things if the worst happens.

Academic issues

Many issues may seem insurmountable but will have a solution. Finding yourself on the wrong level of an English course can often be resolved. Academic issues can be discussed with university staff or a personal tutor; in some cases, support with study skills will resolve the problem. Strategies can be put in place to tackle the difficulties of adjusting and homesickness.

Financial issues

Unfortunately, financial issues are more difficult to address. It is very difficult to find sponsorship and funding once you are in the UK. It is your responsibility to be adequately financially prepared before you come to the UK. If you are not and you don't have enough money to continue, you may have to go home, although there may be opportunities for you to return to study at a later date.

Other unexpected financial issues can befall students, such as problems in a family business or currency issues at home. Whatever the situation, you should speak to your institution as soon as you can. They can advise whether anything can be done and help you to take appropriate action that will not breach visa restrictions.

It is worth considering beforehand whether you will be financially protected in the event of a crisis. Check what your insurance policy will cover. Some policies reimburse fees if you have to leave the course due to illness or accident.

Making a complaint about your institution

You may find yourself in the unfortunate position of being dissatisfied with the institution where you are studying. The first step may be to discuss the matter informally with a member of staff, to see if the issues can be resolved. If you prefer (and if you have one), you can use the service of your students' union. If you need to take things to a more formal level, check your institution's formal procedure for registering complaints. You may have to write a letter or complete a form giving details of the problems; the institution will then have a timescale in which to respond.

If you have not been able to resolve the issues through the methods listed above, you can consider approaching the appropriate external body for your institution. For details, see UKCISA's leaflet *Complaints against your institution*.

A positive outcome

Whatever your cultural background, asking for help is not an admission of failure in the UK; it can often pave the way for a positive outcome, rather than a disaster. Most students have a good experience here in the UK and are very satisfied with their education. According to the International Student Barometer study carried out by i-graduate in 2011: "Overall international student satisfaction remains high at 81%." The same survey shows that satisfaction with support services has increased to 89% (up 15% since 2006). The good news is that if you are in need, then one of the UK's strengths is the support you will receive. You just have to ask.

STUDENT STORY
Alexa Johnson, US

Alexa Johnson, from Idaho in the US, was all set to start her undergraduate studies at a small, liberal arts college in the States, but decided to defer her place so she could travel for a year. Along the way, her plans changed. "In my travels I met so many wonderful people from all around the world, and many of them were from the UK. I fell in love with travelling and some of my British friends suggested that I look into attending university in the UK. They talked me through the UCAS system, I applied, and they quickly accepted my offer.

"I wasn't able to visit the universities before I decided, so I simply read as much as I could about each of them. I knew I wanted to be in London, which was the perfect place for me to be as a creative writer, and I loved the look of the Greenwich campus. Their programme sounded like what I was looking for as well.

"I have always loved to write, even when I was very little. One thing I loved about the UK higher educational experience was the in-depth level of study in one field. I know this type of system isn't a good fit for everybody, but it was a great fit for me because all I wanted to do was write and hone my craft. I was so excited to be able to spend all three years writing, without having to take the basic level classes as you do in a liberal arts system."

Alexa found the UCAS application process a little confusing to start with. "At first, I figured it would be more or less like the US system. I had a friend talk me through the basics, and once I knew those, applying was fairly simple. I found it much easier than the application process I undertook when applying to US universities. So much of the application was simply entering grades and writing a brief personal statement that would be sent to all the universities at the same time. It wasn't as specific to each university, there was less writing than US applications and I only needed one recommendation."

She does have a good tip for students who might be applying to a UK university. "Make sure that you are set in your chosen discipline, because you can't switch majors without starting over again completely."

"Applying for the visa was much more difficult than I imagined it would be. My first application was rejected because I didn't provide my original high school diploma, only a copy of it. Make sure when applying for a visa that you send only originals, even if it seems cumbersome or silly to do so. Also, leave plenty of time to apply, as my visa got lost in the mail and we had to track down the truck carrying it and meet them in order to get it in on time."

Alexa found that her tuition fees were comparable to the costs back home. "As an international student I pay much higher fees, but when they are converted back into dollars it equals about the same as I would have paid at a liberal arts college (with my scholarships subtracted). My living expenses are the only thing that is much more expensive. I was really taken aback at just how incredibly expensive everything is in London, though the experience I've had makes the expense worthwhile."

She felt that she could have done with a little more support before she started the course. "I was still very new to the process of international study and was overwhelmed by everything I had to accomplish before I got there, not to mention moving to a new country. I wish the international office had given me more support and guidance. In most cases I just had to figure it out by myself." When she arrived, there were events that she could get involved with to find out more. "I was invited to an international orientation, where I was able to meet other international students. It was helpful in the sense that I understood the campus more, and it was nice to meet other people experiencing what I was experiencing."

Alexa estimates that it took her about a month to fully settle in. "I was constantly learning new things about the culture and the university system. I didn't know as much as I should have before I came over, and I would suggest that students do their research before coming.

"I love the lifestyle of the UK. At first it can be a bit disconcerting because so many things are similar to the lifestyle in America, but also slightly different. The language is the same, but certain words can be completely confusing. You soon realise that even though it seems like a lot of things are similar to the States, they really are very different. I love British humour, and everyone I have met has been very friendly. It took a little bit of time to get used to the social drinking aspect of the culture, but now I love finding new pubs to visit with friends. Sometimes people can be more reserved and I have to tone down my 'Americanisms', but people are quick to open up." She struggles to come up with any negative experiences around studying in London. "No! Well, perhaps taking the tube in rush hour ..."

She describes some of the differences she encountered in the UK education system. "The classes are year long, and most of them will be in your chosen discipline. I was able to take one elective each year, but these had to be within the same department I was already in (Humanities) so I dabbled in English literature and History classes. Learning is much more focussed on independent study, and you are expected to do much of the outside research on your own. Often I won't have any course work to turn in until the very end of the year, so even though homework isn't due throughout the course, it's vital that independent work is done on a regular basis; otherwise it is very overwhelming at the end of the year. Exams and final projects can be up to 80% of the whole grade for the year, so missing class isn't a good idea. I think that you need a lot more self-discipline in the UK system."

Alexa does feel that she underestimated the cost of living in London. "Food, travel, internet, rent … the list goes on and on. In this city you don't get much for your money, so it's important to be prepared for that. I also learned that it's important not to constantly convert the pounds to dollars, because it is just too depressing (buying lunch for 8 pounds, then realizing that I spent about 14 dollars on a sandwich). I take out the cash I have available to spend for the week and divide it up into categories (£20 for my Oyster travel card, £30 for food, etc). Then I'm not tempted to use my card for anything frivolous or lose track of how much I'm spending.

"Again, food is expensive. I had to learn how to budget pretty quickly. I learned to only eat out once a week and I tried to cook as much as I could. I only shopped at places like Asda and avoided more expensive supermarkets such as Marks & Spencer."

She has been able to work and has been building up her international work experience. "On a student visa I'm allowed to work 20 hours per week during term time and 40 hours per week during vacation periods. My first year in the UK I didn't spend much time looking for a job, because I wanted to get to know people and spend time on my coursework as well as seeing London and the rest of the UK. Near the end of the year I did a one-month work experience internship at a publishing company, which was amazing. There are a lot of work experience opportunities in London at incredible companies, and it's a good way to get a foot in the door. The second year my funds were really dwindling, so I applied for jobs through my university. Most universities have jobshops, and if you sign up for the emails you are kept updated on available jobs. I applied to be a Student Ambassador and got the job! University employment is great because they pay good wages and the jobs are usually fun, but you also gain valuable experience. I was also able to secure an internship at Fulbright after volunteering at their London office. Volunteering and unpaid work experience can lead to other positions, so I would suggest that students sign up to volunteer around the city as often as possible. The last year of university I continued at Fulbright but started work in the University library. I have found that jobs are available for students who work hard and keep on top of what is available."

Alexa is hoping to stay on in the UK after she completes her Bachelor's degree. "I am planning on applying for another student visa for this coming year, as I am doing a master's in London." So, what have been the highlights of her time here so far? "The people, the culture, and living in such a thriving city that is the hub of so many events. The history of the UK is incredible, and still astounds me."

Leeds Trinity University College

Leeds Trinity University College is a small, publicly-funded Higher Education institution with approximately 3,000 students. It is located on a peaceful campus with accommodation, academic and social facilities close to hand, just 6 miles from the centre of Leeds. Leeds has excellent transport links and can be reached by air via Leeds/Bradford Airport or by train – just two hours from London and one and a half hours from Manchester.

Leeds Trinity is teaching-led and has performed consistently well in all external inspections. Innovative programmes are coupled with excellent teaching methods and educational resources. The percentage of students who successfully complete their courses is almost second to none among British universities. Consistently over 50% of our graduates achieve 2.i or 1st class honours degrees.

A wide range of courses are offered at undergraduate and postgraduate levels in Business & Management, Marketing, Education, English, Film Studies, Sport, Health & Leisure, History, Media, Journalism, Psychology, Theology, etc. Our International Foundation programme in conjunction with Twin (www.twinuk.co.uk) leads to a degree course at Leeds Trinity or one of many other universities also recognising the qualification.

A key feature of all our courses is professional content, practical experience and career-focussed learning. We maintain strong links with business, industry and schools, offering professional work placements. 94% of our graduates are in work or further study within six months of graduating.

Tuition fees information can be found at: www.leedstrinity.ac.uk/ International. Part scholarships are offered to eligible international students based on academic merits.

Contact: International Office (international@leedstrinity.ac.uk), Leeds Trinity University College, Brownberrie Lane, Horsforth, Leeds LS18 5HD, UK; www.leedstrinity.ac.uk.

66 At Leeds Trinity, because it's not a massive university, the class sizes are smaller, and you really get to develop an individual relationship with your tutors. You really are a name, not a number, here. 99

Hitesh Sharma, BA Business, Leeds Trinity University College

Chapter 13
After your studies

Just as you need to research and plan your options when you come to the UK to study, the completion of your studies and next steps need to be considered carefully too. You are probably reading this book as preparation for starting your studies in the UK, so thinking about finishing might seem a long way off, but how you move on will partly determine the benefit you gain from your UK experience. If study in the UK is a key part of your education and career, then what you do next should be too.

Leaving the UK

If you have decided to leave the UK, there are various practical considerations. You will need to give notice in advance to your landlord and arrange for the return of any deposit. Contact the suppliers of services such as utilities and telephone. Notify your insurance providers. Find out the cheapest way to send any items home and let people know your change of address. It is useful to leave a forwarding address for outstanding mail. If you had to register with the police, you should return the registration certificate.

You will need to tie up all the loose ends in your financial affairs by paying all outstanding bills and claiming any money owed to you in wages or returned income tax. Cancel all direct debits and standing orders and let your bank know that you will be leaving.

It can take a week or two to close a bank account, so make sure you have access to money in the interim period.

You are likely to need references or testimonials from academic staff or employers. It is a lot easier to get these when you are in the UK rather than trying to do it long distance.

Looking for work outside of the UK

If you will be looking for work when you return home, you should start the research process beforehand. Find out about the opportunities by reading country profiles on the Prospects website at www.prospects.ac.uk. It has links to where to find jobs, as well as explaining the types of opportunities and any pitfalls. You can also use your network of contacts at home to find out about local opportunities.

The careers service at your institution will have information and will be able to support you through this process. Career advisers can help you with decision-making, give insight into jobs and types of work, help you to find activities that will make you more employable and generally enable you to maximise your potential. Go and talk to them early in your studies to ensure you apply at the right time and that you are ready for the application process. Don't expect careers advisers in the UK to tell you what to do or to decide on your future direction; rather, their job is to help you think through your own ideas and support you to make decisions.

Focus on the many skills you have developed; you will have broadened your cultural awareness, developed specific academic and personal skills, and improved your language skills. Studying abroad shows motivation and initiative, but you will have many more transferable skills from studies, work and other activities you have undertaken. Spend some time highlighting your strengths and thinking about what you have to offer, ready for the time when you will need to sell yourself to a potential employer.

Returning home

It might be hard to imagine, but some students experience a kind of reverse culture shock when they return home. It is worth being ready for this somewhat surprising possibility, as it may affect how you relate to friends, family and colleagues and how you adjust to life back home. Some universities offer information sessions to help you prepare. Bear in mind that the skills you honed to help you adapt to the UK can also be used as you return home or move to another country; the experience should have provided you with at least two more skills to add to your CV: flexibility and adaptability.

Further study in the UK

If you are an international student intending to continue with further studies, you will need to apply for an extension to your visa. Make a note of the date when your visa expires and make contact with your international office at least four months before this date; this should give you ample time to prepare the application. If you wait until after your visa expires to apply, you may be subject to an automatic ban from the UK due to overstaying.

Your university or college will be able to help you with the process of researching and applying for further study within the UK.

Working in the UK

Students from the EEA can generally stay on and work in the UK without issue, although there are some conditions applying to those from accession countries. See the UK Border Agency website for further details at www.ukba.homeoffice. gov.uk/eucitizens.

The options for international students to work in the UK have changed recently under new immigration rules. If you intend to apply to stay on and work, you need to research your options well before your visa expires.

Those graduating with a degree (or postgraduate certificate or diploma in education) can be considered for employment under the Tier 2 (skilled worker) route if they apply from the UK before the expiration of their visa. You will need an employer and a job offer meeting minimum salary requirements before you can apply. Essentially, any job will have to be a graduate-level shortage occupation and the employer must have a Tier 2 licence, although only a limited number of employers do. You can find the current register of sponsors online, although inclusion on the list doesn't mean that they are currently recruiting. Find out more from your university's international office or at www.ukba. homeoffice.gov.uk/visas-immigration/working/tier2/general.

Consideration will be given to student entrepreneurs with strong business ideas who plan to stay on in the UK.

> ❝ The new visa restrictions unfortunately make it difficult to stay on and work in the UK if you're not from an EU country. ❞
>
> *Alexandra Kamins, US*

Talk to your careers service for further information and support in looking for work in the UK.

Keeping in touch

After you leave, you will still want to keep in contact with your friends and colleagues. Many students join a university or college alumni organisation to maintain a link with the institution and keep up to date with events and developments. Many services of the university will still be available to you after you leave, including careers services. The British Council also holds information on events for UK alumni in your home country at www.britishcouncil.org.

Richmond University

Marine Strauss

Marine came from France to study a BA in International Relations at Richmond University. Richmond's large and diverse international student body made it an obvious choice, and Marine has made lifelong friends and connections from around the world during her studies. Richmond has also given Marine the opportunity to gain both an American and British accredited degree without having to travel to America.

Now in her final year of study, Marine undertook a summer internship in Cambodia at an NGO that helps to prevent human trafficking. The internship blends her undergraduate study of International Relations with her personal interest in Human and Children's Rights.

"I will get to do what I want to do, and work in what is really interesting to me," said Marine about her upcoming experience. "I know that the language barrier, different culture and workload will be challenging and demanding, but this is going to be an incredible, life-changing experience. Parts of my family are from Cambodia, so this is going to be both a personal and professional journey."

Marine credits Richmond for equipping her with the skills to meet the challenges of an ever-changing world. Her experiences both in and out of class have meant that she is constantly considering the diverse needs of different people and cultures. Building a strong and lasting network of like-minded thinkers who will help drive her future career forward in the NGO sector.

Find out more about studying at Richmond at
www.richmond.ac.uk
enroll@richmond.ac.uk
+44 (0)208 332 9000

The last word

Choosing to study overseas is a brave, and sometimes challenging, path to take. However, if you choose wisely from the options available to you in the UK, you should find your bravery rewarded with an exceptional educational experience and a wealth of new skills. At the end of your time here, you will be able to show employers and universities not only your UK qualifications, but also the ways in which you have developed from immersing yourself in another culture, not to mention making lifelong friends, broadening your horizons and improving your English. The UK is known all over the world for its education; now you have a chance to be part of it.

> ❝ My experience here has been like no other. I have gained responsibility and have become more organised with everything that I do. Now I truly feel like a young adult. ❞
>
> *Bola Phillips, Nigeria*

66 It's good to go to another country, to learn many things, not only the language but culture from all over the world. I have learned many things I couldn't learn in Japan. I have met people from all over the world. 99

Minami Eto, Japan

66 If you study in the UK you have the possibility to improve your English. This is a very important thing to do as it's the most important language in the world nowadays. You have the possibility to grow up a lot as you live on your own; you have to solve the little problems of everyday life without the help of your parents. 99

Erica Cancelli, Italy

66 When it comes to science, at school and university, the UK has a great way of teaching, as there are a lot of demonstrations, practical work and hands-on experiments, making the subject very interesting and exciting. 99

Yana Dautova, Russia

66 The people, the culture and living in such a thriving city that is the hub of so many events have been my highlights here. 99

Alexa Johnson, US

> 66 The experience itself is the best thing about studying in the UK. 99
>
> *Cynthia Cheah, Malaysia*

> 66 From my own experience, the best things about studying here are the open and friendly environment and the many awesome friends I made during my years here. 99
>
> *David Stoll, Luxembourg*

> 66 The best things are the diversity of the people I have met and the true friends I have made. I am so pleased that I chose to continue my studies here and my English is now much stronger. Studying here has changed my life. 99
>
> *Andrzej Polewiak, Poland*

> 66 I have learned so much more about myself and my country in one year than I had in the previous 21 years combined. I have met the most inspiring people and I have made connections all over Europe that I know will serve me for the rest of my life and career. The UK has an international presence that is unparalleled by any other country in Europe. 99
>
> *Kimberly Stevenson, US*

Further research

Top three websites for studying in the UK

UKCISA (UK Council for International Student Affairs):
www.ukcisa.org.uk
British Council website for education in the UK:
www.educationuk.org
UK Border Agency: www.ukba.homeoffice.gov.uk

Finding out about the UK

VisitBritain: www.visitbritain.com
VisitEngland: www.visitengland.org
VisitScotland: www.visitscotland.com
VisitWales: www.visitwales.com
Discover Northern Ireland: www.discovernorthernireland.com

University groups

Russell Group: www.russellgroup.ac.uk
1994 Group: www.1994group.ac.uk
University Alliance: www.unialliance.ac.uk
million+: www.millionplus.ac.uk
ukadia: www.ukadia.ac.uk

Finding and applying for a course

English UK: www.englishuk.com/en/students
Search for English language courses in the UK

Ofqual: www.ofqual.gov.uk
Includes regulated qualifications and awarding organisations

Education UK: www.educationuk.org
Search for UK courses, institutions and scholarships

Prospects: www.prospects.ac.uk
Graduate careers website, including a postgraduate course search

Find a master's: www.findamasters.com
Search for master's degrees

Find a PhD: www.findaphd.com
Search for PhDs

UCAS: www.ucas.com
Course search and online application for most undergraduate courses

UKPASS: www.ukpass.ac.uk
Postgraduate course search; application to some universities

CUKAS: www.cukas.ac.uk
Course search and online application for conservatoires

GTTR: www.gttr.ac.uk
Course search and online application for postgraduate teacher training

UK NARIC: www.naric.org.uk

Compare your qualifications to the UK qualifications frameworks

Useful books

How to Complete Your UCAS Application 2013 entry, Beryl
Dixon, Trotman.

How to Write a Winning UCAS Personal Statement, Ian Stannard,
Trotman.

Practise & Pass Professional: LNAT, Georgina Petrova and
Christopher M. Reid, Trotman.

Practise & Pass Professional: Numeracy Tests, Alan Redman,
Trotman.

Practise & Pass Professional: Verbal Reasoning Tests, Alan
Redman, Trotman.

Inspection, accreditation and quality

Ofsted: www.ofsted.gov.uk
Inspection of schools and colleges in England

Education Scotland: www.educationscotland.gov.uk/
inspectionandreview/
Inspection of schools and colleges in Scotland

Estyn: www.estyn.gov.uk
Inspection of schools and colleges in Wales

ETI: www.etini.gov.uk
Inspection of schools and colleges in Northern Ireland

Independent Schools Inspectorate: www.isi.net
Inspection of independent schools

British Accreditation Council: www.the-bac.org
Accreditation for private further and higher education

Accreditation Service for International Colleges:
www.asic.org.uk
Accreditation for private international colleges

Association of British Language Schools: www.abls.co.uk
Accreditation for private language schools

Research Assessment Exercise: www.rae.ac.uk
Reports on the quality of research at higher education institutions

Unistats: http://unistats.direct.gov.uk
Student satisfaction surveys

iAgora: www.iagora.com/studies/United_Kingdom
Study abroad experiences and opinions

University league tables

Complete University Guide:
www.thecompleteuniversityguide.co.uk
The Times: www.thetimes.co.uk
Guardian: www.guardian.co.uk/education/universityguide
Times Higher Education (worldwide): www.timeshighereducation.
co.uk/world-university-rankings/
Academic Ranking of World Universities (worldwide):
www.arwu.org
QS Top University (worldwide): www.topuniversities.com
FT Business School Rankings (worldwide): www.ft.com/
businesseducation/mba

Study exchanges

British Council: www.britishcouncil.org/erasmus.htm
Exchanges within the EU

Fulbright Commission: www.fulbright.co.uk
Exchanges from the US

Erasmus Mundus: http://ec.europa.eu/education/external-relation-programmes/mundus_en.htm
Offering Europe joint master's and doctorates with scholarships

International universities with a UK campus

Global Higher Education: www.globalhighered.org/branchcampuses.php

Distance learning in the UK

Open and Distance Learning Quality Council: www.odlqc.org.uk
The Open University: www.open.ac.uk

Funding and scholarships

Website of the UK government: www.direct.gov.uk
Information for EU students studying in England

Student Awards Agency for Scotland: www.saas.gov.uk
Information for EU students studying in Scotland

Student Finance Wales: www.studentfinancewales.co.uk
Information for EU students studying in Wales

niDirect: www.nidirect.gov.uk
Information for EU students studying in Northern Ireland

Commonwealth Scholarship and Fellowship Plan: www.csfp-online.org

Chevening Scholarships: www.facebook.com/officialchevening

Marshall Scholarships: www.marshallscholarship.org

9/11 Scholarships: www.britishcouncil.org/911scholarships.htm

Fulbright Awards Programme: www.fulbright.co.uk

Newton International Fellowships: www.newtonfellowships.org

Gates Cambridge Scholarships: www.gatesscholar.org

Mitchell Scholars Programme: www.us-irelandalliance.org

Rhodes Scholarships: www.rhodeshouse.ox.ac.uk

Saltire Scholarships: www.talentscotland.com/students/study/scholarships/saltire-scholarships.aspx

Research Council funding: www.rcuk.ac.uk

Education UK: www.educationuk.org
Search for scholarships

Scholarship Search: www.scholarship-search.org.uk
Search for scholarships

Prospects: www.prospects.ac.uk/funding
Sources of funding for further study

Students with disabilities

Disability Rights UK: www.disabilityrightsuk.org/
disabledstudents.htm
Information for students with disabilities

Higher Education Accessibility Guides (HEAG): www.european-
agency.org/agency-projects/heag
Guide to disability support services at EU universities, including
the UK

Immigration and visas

UK Border Agency: www.ukba.homeoffice.gov.uk

UKCISA: www.ukcisa.org.uk
The UKCISA website includes information sheets on immigration
and visas

British Foreign and Commonwealth Office (ATAS): www.fco.gov.
uk/en/about-us/what-we-do/services-we-deliver/atas
Guidelines on the ATAS certificate; whether you will need one and
how to apply

Preparing for UK study

Prepare for Success: www.prepareforsuccess.org.uk
Learning tool to prepare for UK study

Living costs and budgeting

International UNIAID Student Calculator: www.studentcalculator.
org.uk/international/
Prepare for the financial side of UK study and set a budget

MoneySupermarket: www.moneysupermarket.com
Money-saving tips and comparison of costs, including insurance
and mobile phone providers

TV Licensing: www.tvlicensing.co.uk
Find out whether you'll need a TV licence

mySupermarket: www.mysupermarket.co.uk
Find the best deals on supermarket prices

Department of Health: www.dh.gov.uk
Find out whether you'll get free NHS treatment

Housing

Shelter England: http://england.shelter.org.uk
Advice and your rights around housing in England

Shelter Scotland: http://scotland.shelter.org.uk
Advice and your rights around housing in Scotland

Shelter Cymru: www.sheltercymru.org.uk
Advice and your rights around housing in Wales

Housing Advice NI: www.housingadviceni.org
Advice and your rights around housing in Northern Ireland

Travel

International Student Identity Card: www.isiccard.com
Gain student discounts overseas with an ISIC

Travel within the UK
The Trainline: www.thetrainline.com
Train travel within the UK

16–25 Railcard: www.16-25railcard.co.uk

Raileasy: www.raileasy.co.uk
Rail travel (including Northern Ireland)

National Express: www.nationalexpress.com
National Express coach travel

Megabus: http://uk.megabus.com
Megabus coach travel

Translink: www.translink.co.uk
Travel within Northern Ireland

European and worldwide travel

Skyscanner: www.skyscanner.net
Search for cheap flights

KAYAK: www.kayak.com
Search for cheap flights

TravelSupermarket: www.travelsupermarket.com
Search for cheap flights

Eurolines: www.eurolines.co.uk
Scheduled coach travel across Europe

InterRail: www.interrailnet.com
Fixed-price rail travel across Europe

Eurail: www.eurail.com
Fixed-price rail travel across Europe

Ferry Savers: www.ferrysavers.co.uk
Search for cheap ferry tickets

Eurotunnel: www.eurotunnel.com
Eurotunnel between UK and France

STA Travel: www.statravel.co.uk
Travel specialists for young people

Somewhere to stay while travelling

Hostelling International: www.hihostels.com
Youth Hostel Associations across the world

HostelBookers: www.hostelbookers.com
Search for hostel accommodation

HostelWorld: www.hostelworld.com
Search for hostel accommodation

CouchSurfing: www.couchsurfing.org
Hospitality network with free accommodation

The Hospitality Club: www.hospitalityclub.org
Hospitality network with free accommodation

Glossary

A levels
General Certificate of Education Advanced Level qualifications; a pre-university qualification in the UK

Access to Higher Education (HE) Diploma
A course offering a route to university for adults without the usual qualifications

.ac.uk
Web domain name for post-compulsory education providers in the UK

Advanced Higher
Advanced qualifications that encourage independent learning; these can be taken as an option after Highers in Scotland

AS levels
General Certificate of Education Advanced Subsidiary Level qualifications; year one of the two-year A level

ATAS
Academic Technology Approval Scheme

Bedsit
A single room with sleeping, living and often cooking facilities in a single space

Bologna Process

A European reform of higher education to enable student mobility

British Council

The organisation dealing with the UK's international cultural relations and promoting opportunities for UK study

BTEC Diploma

Work-related qualification combining theory and applied learning

CAS

Confirmation of Acceptance for Studies; this number is needed to apply for a visa

CEFR

Common European Framework of Reference for languages

Conditional offer

An offer of a place at an institution that depends on the student meeting certain conditions

Conservatoire

A centre for excellence in dance, drama or music

CRB

Criminal Records Bureau or police check; required if working or volunteering with children or vulnerable adults

CUKAS

Conservatoires UK Admissions Service

Direct debit

An authorisation set up by the bank account holder allowing money to be taken from the account, often for bills

Dissertation
An original piece of research, often submitted as part of a taught degree

ECTS
European Credit Transfer System

EGAS
Educational Grants Advisory Service

EHEA
European Higher Education Area; the countries where the Bologna process is utilised

EHIC
European Health Insurance Card

Erasmus
European Union exchange programme for higher education

ESOL
English for Speakers of Other Languages

FHEQ
Framework for Higher Education Qualifications

Freshers' week
A student's first week at university involving orientation events, the chance to join clubs and societies, meet friends and attend parties

GCSE
General Certificate of Secondary Education

Grants Register
A worldwide guide to postgraduate funding

GTTR
Graduate Teacher Training Registry

HEAR
The Higher Education Achievement Report is issued at graduation and provides detailed information about a student's achievements

HESA
Higher Education Statistics Agency

Higher
Scottish national qualification often studied as a route to higher education

Higher education institution
Any university or college offering higher education qualifications

Highly Trusted Sponsor
The status required to enable an institution to issue a CAS

Homestay
Accommodation option that involves lodging with a host family

IELTS
International English Language Testing System

International Baccalaureate
A two-year programme of education for 16–19 year olds which encourages breadth of learning and an international perspective; the IB is a pre-university qualification

Inventory
An itemised list of a property and its contents

ISIC
International Student Identity Card

NHS
National Health Service

NINo
National Insurance Number; this number is needed for work

NQF
National Qualifications Framework

NUS
National Union of Students

OISC
Office of the Immigration Services Commissioner

Ofqual
Office of Qualifications and Examinations Regulation; the
regulator of qualifications and exams in England

Packed lunch
Food that you prepare to take to your place of work or study

PET
Preliminary English Test

Polytechnic
A higher education institution for technical and vocational learning

PTE
Pearson Test of English

QAA
Quality Assurance Agency for Higher Education

QCF
Qualifications and Credit Framework

RAE
Research Assessment Exercise

REF
Research Excellence Framework

Research proposal
A document explaining the nature of your research and how you will carry it out

Russell Group
Twenty-four leading universities working together to maintain the best standards of research and outstanding teaching

SCQF
Scottish Credit and Qualifications Framework

SELT
Secure English Language Test

Standard Grades
Scottish qualifications taken at age 15 or 16; comparable to GCSEs in the rest of the UK

Thesis
An original piece of research, often forming the basis of a research-based degree

Tier 2

Skilled worker visa under the points-based system

Tier 4

Student visa under the points-based system

TOEFL iBT

Test of English as a Foreign Language (internet-based test)

UCAS

Universities and Colleges Admissions Service; responsible for managing applications to higher education courses

UK Border Agency

The border control body of the UK government

UK NARIC

UK National Academic Recognition Information Centre; the official source of information on international qualifications

UKCISA

UK Council for International Student Affairs; the national advisory body for international students

UKPASS

UK Postgraduate Application and Statistical Service; this organisation processes applications for a number of universities

Unconditional offer

An offer of a place at an institution with no academic conditions

Viva voce

An oral examination

Index of advertisers